DINING WITH
PROUST

Published in 1992 by Ebury Press
an imprint of Random House UK Ltd
Random House
20 Vauxhall Bridge Road
London SW1V 2SA

French edition, *Proust La Cuisine Retrouvée* by Anne Borrel, Alain
Senderens and Jean-Bernard Naudin, first published in 1991 by
Société Nouvelle des Éditions du Chêne

Translated by Wendy Allatson, Simon Knight, Sue Rose, Isabel
Varea, Ros Schwartz (coordinator)

Typeset in Garamond 3 by Textype Typesetters, Cambridge
Printed and bound in Italy

A catalogue record for this book is available from the British
Library

ISBN 0 09 177506 X

Important note: *All recipe measurements give the Imperial
amount first, followed by the metric and then the U.S. equivalent.
As these are not exact equivalents, please work from one set of
figures. U.S. teaspoons, tablespoons, pints, quarts and gallons
are all smaller than Imperial ones.*

*If you cannot find crème fraîche, a good substitute is two parts
heavy cream mixed with one part sour cream.*

DINING WITH
PROUST

Anne BORREL
Alain SENDERENS
Jean-Bernard NAUDIN

Design
Nanou BILLAULT

Series editor
Marie-France BOYER

with the collaboration of
Agnès CARBONELL

EBURY PRESS · LONDON

ACKNOWLEDGEMENTS

I am glad of this opportunity to thank all those who have had a hand in the creation of this book and have lent their support and encouragement: M. Maurice Schumann of the Académie Française, chairman of the Amis de Marcel Proust; Dr. Michel Haroche, who first pointed out the affinity between the cuisine of Proust and that of Aristotle; Mme Claire Joyes and M. Jean-Marie Toulgouat, authors of *Les Carnets de cuisine de Claude Monet,* whose help and advice was invaluable; and M. Pierre Marchesseau, who supported me in the early stages.

I am also grateful to those who have contributed their specialized knowledge: Mme Geneviève Baudon and the Librairie Gourmande; Mme Nanou Billault, whose inspired research helped us recreate the décor of a byegone age; Mme Gisèle Bohan, faithful servant of the Musée Marcel Proust at Illiers-Combray; M. Jacques Bontillot, curator of the Musée de la Faïnce (pottery museum) at Montereau; M. and Mme Alban Bouniol de Gineste of the Château de Réveillon; M. Ralph Brauner; M. David Campbell; M. and Mme Jean Frémont of les Aigneaux, Illiers-Combray; M. Bertrand Guéneron and the Lucas-Carton restaurant; M. Louis Monier; Dr. Reiner Speck, chairman of the Proust Gesellschaft, Cologne; and Alain Senderens, whose knowledge of Proust, creative genius and diligence, perfectly combined, are a recipe for true poetry.

Anne Borrel

I would like to record my gratitude to everyone who worked on the photographs for this book.

My thanks go, firstly, to Nanou Billault, without whose enthusiasm, skills and painstaking approach the project would not have been possible.

Secondly, I am grateful to Anne-Françoise Pelissier and Jean-Jacques Aubert, whose amiability, cheerfulness and dynamism have facilitated an at times difficult task.

Lastly, I wish to stress that these pictures are no more than a subjective interpretation of the world of Marcel Proust – a world which, though relatively recent, remains singularly elusive.

Jean-Bernard Naudin

CONTENTS

9

PREFACE

11

FOREWORD

15

THE TASTES OF CHILDHOOD
Auteuil to Illiers, Illiers to Combray

43

THE LADY IN PINK
The Swann household in Paris

55

THE MILITARY PARADISE
Orléans to Doncières

65

MME VERDURIN'S WEDNESDAYS
Paris and la Raspelière

81

HIGH SOCIETY
Réveillon to Guermantes

99

THE SEA
Cabourg to Balbec

117

DINING WITH PROUST

133

THE RECIPES

188

INDEX

190

SELECT BIBLIOGRAPHY

191

SOURCES OF QUOTATIONS

PREFACE

I am greatly honoured that Anne Borrel and Les Editions du Chêne should have chosen me for the task of recreating the dishes beloved of Marcel Proust, references to which feature so prominently in his writings. As we explore the culinary delights of his great novel, we become aware of the creative alchemy whereby reality is transmuted into art.

Many writers draw on the higher senses of sight and hearing, on intuition and discernment; but few venture into the realms of touch, smell and taste. Often, these senses find expression only in writings in the comic mode: they have been banished from serious literature since the seventeenth century, which saw a divorce of body and soul, spirit and matter. In using culinary imagery, Proust re-establishes contact with a time-honoured tradition, sustained by great philosophers – from Pythagoras to Rabelais – and famous writers, who were not above illustrating their poetic or learned discourse with references to food, taste and the art of cookery.

Although the dinner table may be the womb of culture par excellence, the literature discussed over the meal rarely appeals to the masses. It is the genius of Marcel Proust that he makes the down-to-earth topic of food an appropriate, if not the ideal, vehicle for understanding the cultural sub-conscious of the Western world.

Again and again, he leads us from the realm of the senses to the realm of ideas, from the sensual, if not explicitly sexual, domain to the domain of food. His delight in the well-seasoned epithet, a full-flavoured turn of phrase and the vibrancy of his landscapes elevate his memories to a higher plane. Far from suppressing the sense of taste, Proust demonstrates that food is the key to our inner enigmas, transporting us into the labyrinths of our intimate mythological world; it is the very stuff of imagination, like a built-in code-book of secret symbols. To decipher the mystery concealed behind the veil in the holy of holies of the unconscious, Proust draws on the cooking of Françoise – his personal key to the past.

As well as a harmonious depiction of a complex inner world, Proust's work is a valuable record of the way a kitchen was run, the planning of meals and menus, the tastes of the Belle Epoque, and the author's own culinary predilections.

In the early years of the century, technical innovations, such as gas, electricity and refrigeration, together with the introduction of new products, brought a revolution to the kitchen – changing people's lives even more than have recent developments in the way food is prepared and served. There was a severing of links with the country and the provincial way of life of earlier generations, and eating habits changed. Cookery was dragged into the modern age, ceasing to be women's work and becoming the province of the chef and restaurateur.

In *Le Goût du nouveau,* Alberto Capatti noted that there were now more important considerations than the routine visit to the market; there was a confusing mixture of old and new, with familiar items missing from the shopping basket. The conflict of the new age might have been summed up in the phrase: for or against technology. At the same time, the first banana made its appearance at Hédiard's – the sales girls having to explain that this fruit from paradise must be eaten skinned. The Universal Exhibition marked the beginnings of internationalism in gastronomy, opening up new areas previously restricted to the élite. People flocked to pavilions lit by gas and electricity, and to see the sterilizers used for producing tinned foods. The art of cookery was dying; real food was dead. There was widespread pessimism among gourmets and, in 1912, Proust wrote of the collapse in culinary standards. In 1914, he joined in the general chorus of dismay, giving up croissants with his *café au lait* because it was impossible to find a baker making the genuine article. Similarly, the savour of *boeuf mode* as prepared by his parents' cook was no more than a fond memory.

There was also a good deal of scepticism about the quality of food. While gourmets refused to have anything to do with refrigeration, the veterinary surgeons responsible for policing the Paris markets revealed that seizures of rotten meat accounted for 40 to 50% of all confiscated produce.

In *Against Sainte-Beuve,* written during this period of gastronomic upheaval, Proust commented that: "What the intellect gives us back under the name of the past is not it. In reality, as happens with the souls of the departed in certain popular legends, each hour of our lives, as soon as it is dead, embodies and conceals itself in some material object. Unless we meet with that object it remains captive there, captive for ever. We recognize it through the object, we summon it, and it is released. We may very well never meet with the object it is concealed in – or with the sensation, since relative to ourselves every object is a sensation."

Whereas for Paul Valéry, "man (is the) measure of all things," for Marcel Proust, taste is the measure and the memory.

Monsieur Proust, master of the sense of taste, I bring alive these recipes of your time.

Alain SENDERENS

FOREWORD

What a pleasure to cook for oneself... These words in one of Marcel Proust's notebooks reveal an unexpected facet of the great writer's personality. Appreciative of good food and himself an attentive host, he had an instinctive feel for what was genuine and wholesome. Not wishing to miss any aspect of the rich world of the senses, he tasted food in the same way as, since childhood, he had devoured good books. And, in his work, he established a parity between writer and chef: *"I abandoned myself with delight to the pleasure of composing sentences, like a cook who, free for once of having to cook for others, at last finds time to enjoy his food."*

His sensitivity, as well as his sensuality, led Proust towards the truth of art. Before embarking on his great work, he wrote: *"Daily I attach less value to the intellect."* Forgotten smells and tastes are rediscovered through the *true intelligence, the intelligence of the heart.*

Proust had long realized that the simplest dishes are the most difficult to prepare, and what was true of cooking was true of other arts: *"A biftek aux pommes, the ideal competition piece, difficult by its very simplicity, a sort of* Sonate Pathétique *of cooking."* A demanding school of modesty and truth, the kitchen was a place of secret alchemies.

Because, for Proust, *"real life, life at last laid bare and illuminated – the only life in consequence which can be said to be really lived – is literature,"* this book explores his writings on food, following the times and seasons of his life. Visiting the places once frequented by the writer – Illiers, Réveillon, Cabourg – or the settings evoked in his work, *Dining with Proust* restores to us a time, a lifestyle, tastes and flavours which seemed impossible to recapture.

Drawing on his knowledge of Proust's work, tradition and his own genius, Alain Senderens has resurrected recipes from the past, bringing us the culinary delights of the Belle Epoque.

Anne Borrel

THE TASTES OF CHILDHOOD

"Certainly my mother's beautiful face seemed to shine again with youth that evening, as she sat gently holding my hands and trying to check my tears..."
Portrait of Mme Proust in 1880, by Mme Beauvais. (Left)

"There is, following an ample meal, a sort of pause in time, a gentle slackening of thought and energy, when to sit doing nothing gives us a sense of life's richness..." (Opposite)

"... When from a long-distant past nothing subsists, (...) taste and smell alone remain poised a long time, like souls (...) and bear unflinchingly, in the tiny and almost impalpable drop of their essence, the vast structure of recollection." (Right)

Cocooned in his cork-lined room, the writer feverishly filled the pages of exercise books. Sometimes he would invite his friends out to dine in the middle of the night, offering them lavish suppers which he hardly touched. What did he live on in his self-imposed reclusion and what sustained him? Writing, a feast of words of which there would apparently always be an abundant supply. His was a life overflowing with scents and flavours, a life fulfilled by its own richness.

The recluse of the boulevard Haussmann recalled his life in a wealth of delightful detail. He would find the exact shade of meaning to describe a hawthorn hedge and, above all, described memories of delicious dishes in mouthwatering detail. It had all started with a subtle and almost insignificant taste. A simple and subtle taste had suddenly brought memories of childhood flooding back:

One day in winter, on my return home, my mother, seeing that I was cold, offered me some tea, a thing I did not ordinarily take. I declined at first, and then, for no particular reason, changed my mind. She sent for one of those squat, plump little cakes called "petites madeleines," which look as though they had been moulded in the fluted valve of a scallop shell. And soon, mechanically, dispirited after a dreary day with the prospect of a depressing morrow, I raised to my lips a spoonful of the tea in which I had soaked a morsel of cake. No sooner had the warm liquid mixed with the crumbs touched my palate than a shudder ran through me and I stopped, intent upon the extraordinary thing that was happening to me. An exquisite pleasure had invaded my senses, something isolated, detached, with no suggestion of its origin. And at once the vicissitudes of life had become indifferent to me, its disasters innocuous, its brevity illusory — this new sensation having had on me the effect which love has of filling me with a precious essence; or rather this essence was not in me, it was me. I had ceased now to feel mediocre, contingent, mortal. Whence could it have come to me, this all-powerful joy? I sensed that it was connected with the taste of the tea and the cake, (...) And suddenly the memory revealed itself. The taste was that of the little piece of madeleine which on Sunday mornings at Combray (because on those mornings I did not go out before mass), when I went to say good morning to her in her bedroom, my aunt Léonie

"She had to leave ... with my little brother, and as he was leaving the house, my Uncle had taken him to have his photograph done ... They had curled his hair ... , his plump face was framed by a helmet of bouffant black hair ... I gazed at him with the smile of an older child for a much loved brother ..."
Marcel Proust and his "brother in his little frock coat and his lace coat," circa 1878.

used to give me, dipping it first in her own cup of tea or tisane. (...) And as soon as I had recognized the taste of the piece of madeleine soaked in the decoction of lime-blossom which my aunt used to give me (...) immediately the old grey house upon the street, where her room was, rose up like a stage set to attach itself to the little pavilion opening on to the garden which had been built out behind it for my parents (...) and with the house the town, from morning to night and in all weathers, the Square where I used to be sent before lunch, the streets along which I used to run errands, the country roads we took when it was fine. (...) all the flowers in our garden and in M. Swann's park, and the water-lilies on the Vivonne and the good folk of the village and their little dwellings and the parish church and the whole of Combray and its surroundings, taking shape and solidity, sprang into being, town and gardens alike, from my cup of tea. (Swann's Way)

"At one side of her bed stood a big yellow chest-of-drawers of lemon-wood, and a table which served at once as dispensary and high altar, on which, beneath a statue of the Virgin and a bottle of Vichy-Célestins, might be found her prayer-books and her medical pre-scriptions, everything that she needed for the performance, in bed, of her duties to soul and body, to keep the proper times for pepsin and for vespers."

"Bathilde, come in and stop your husband drinking brandy!"
Mme Nathée Weil, née Adèle Berncastel, Marcel Proust's maternal grandmother.

Printed invoice for the Proust-Torcheux grocery business in Illiers, owned by Proust's father's family.

Remembrance of Things Past was written by a sick man who was subjected to an extremely strict diet. Among the lessons it conceals are treatises on taste and style. In the austere atmosphere of his sick room, filled with the vapour of fumigations and so very reminiscent of Tante Léonie's room, Marcel Proust savoured the inexhaustible provender of remembrance. He indulged his taste for the words which gave substance to his memories. His work could be given the subtitle: The Fine Art of Cuisine. The art of living that it describes with such nostalgic sensuality belongs to an age when gastronomic delights formed the very basis of family and society life. It was an age when everyday life was highlighted by meals whose refinement and abundance fire the imagination of the modern reader. These two apparently contradictory qualities are also distinctive features of Proust's style which combines an abundance of imagery with an extreme precision of detail. *Cuisine* is one of the keys to the skilfully ordered labyrinth of *Remembrance of Things Past*.

This flood of childhood memories was immediately linked to that early sense of taste which tends to be neglected in later life. For children, the world is like a vast palace from the *Arabian Nights* where everything, including the intangible, is edible. It is a world in which even Tante Léonie's room becomes something good to eat:

The air of those rooms was saturated with the fine bouquet of a silence so nourishing, so succulent, that I never went into them without a sort of greedy anticipation, particularly on those first mornings, chilly still, of the Easter holidays, when I could taste it more fully because I had only just arrived in Combray (...) while the fire, baking like dough the appetizing smells with which the air of the room was thickly clotted and which the moist and sunny freshness of the morning had already "raised" and started to "set," puffed them and glazed them and fluted them and swelled them into an invisible though not impalpable country pie, an immense "turnover" to which, barely waiting to savour the crisper, more delicate, more reputable but also drier aromas of the cupboard, the chest-of-drawers and the patterned wall-paper, I always returned with an unconfessed gluttony to wallow in the central, glutinous, insipid, indigestible and fruity smell of the flowered bedspread. (Swann's Way)

These "gustative reminiscences" take us behind the scenes of the novel. Proust adopted a culinary approach to the process of literary creation, combining the various ingredients provided by reality, with the result that Combray is in fact a blend of two places, Auteuil and Illiers, where he spent the happiest days of his childhood.

He was born in Auteuil on 10 July 1871 at 96, rue La Fontaine. The house, which belonged to his maternal grandfather, Louis Weil, has since been demolished to make way for the avenue Mozart. In fine weather, the family would sit and talk for hours in the darkness of the garden, their conversations always turning to reminiscences of dinner parties and exchanged recipes for chicken chasseur. The assembled company would include Proust's maternal grandparents, Adèle and Nathée Weil, his Oncle Georges, his cousins on his mother's side of the family and the Crémieux girls who were the daughters and granddaughters of Adolphe Crémieux, a government minister and great man of the family.

Marcel's father spent very little time in this country retreat on the outskirts of Paris. Professor Adrien Proust, a brilliant doctor and senior registrar at the Hôpital de la Charité, was entrusted with numerous official assignments. He lived at 8, rue Roy (boulevard Haussmann) and, after 1873, at 9, boulevard Malesherbes, the successive Paris addresses of the Proust family. But it was during those long, lazy evenings in the garden at Auteuil that the young Proust was best able to enjoy the company of his mother, Jeanne Weil. Provided, of course, that no untimely guests stole her from him or were the cause of his having to go to bed without her goodnight kiss, a drama described in the opening pages of the book. For him, this spiritual food was inseparable from all the other forms of food which were so plentiful at Auteuil and Illiers.

Illiers was the birthplace of the Proust family. Since the 16th century, Marcel's paternal ancestors had been among the worthies of this small market town near Chartres. They were grocers, candle merchants and bailiffs in Illiers. When Adrien Proust, a brilliant scholarship pupil at the lycée in Chartres, decided to go to Paris to study medicine, he was the first member of the family to leave the Beauce region. His father, Louis

"We looked in to tell Théodore to bring a larger brioche than usual because our cousins had taken advantage of the fine weather to come over from Thiberzy for lunch."
Edouard Manet, Still Life with Brioche, Christie's, London.

"It would be my duty to shake out of the chemist's little package on to a plate the amount of lime-blossom required for infusion in boiling water."

"She would hold out for me to kiss her sad, pale, lacklustre forehead, on which at this early hour she would not yet have arranged her false hair."
Illiers: a photograph of Mme Jules Amiot, née Elisabeth Proust (1823-1886), Marcel Proust's aunt.

Proust, had an eye for progress and, with the invention of the stearin candle, had established a prosperous candle factory. Until his death in 1863, he and his wife Virginie Torcheux ran a grocery store in the place du Marché, opposite the church in Illiers, selling haberdashery, crockery, glassware, bottles and crystal ware, nails, brandy and liqueurs. The sign over the shop also indicated that they manufactured wax, honey and candles as well as health chocolate and vanilla chocolate.

Adrien Proust's elder sister, Elisabeth, married Jules Amiot, a landowner and shopkeeper. He owned the draper's shop in the square with the yellow door which reminded Proust of the huge apple tart they used to bring on Sundays.

Marcel Proust used to spend his holidays in the house at 4, rue du Saint-Esprit, owned by his Oncle Jules. Together with the house at Auteuil, it provided the setting for Combray. The magic of this subtle combination gave substance to the intangible and peopled it with characters who were even more real than those who had actually existed.

In the course of *Remembrance of Things Past*, Combray represents Proust's initiation into the art of taste, supervised by a protecting divinity in the person of Françoise, the cook. Her role was distinct from that of the family who were responsible for his initiation into literary and aesthetic taste. Someone from outside the family circle disrupted this early harmony by introducing another type of taste, the "taste" for society and art. And this person was Charles Swann.

Who was Swann? "... *A bald, eloquent, fanciful man and a devotee of the table, who lives by the rule of Brillat-Savarin.*" (*Cities of the Plain*). He was an aesthete who combined the skills of an art critic and a gourmet. This man, who was one of the most sought-after men in the high society of the faubourg Saint-Germain used to relax in the garden at Combray and describe recipes in a wealth of detail. In fact, "*It seemed quite natural, therefore, to send him whenever a recipe for sauce gribiche or for pineapple salad was needed for one of our big dinner-parties, to which he himself would not be invited. (...) this early Swann abounding in leisure, fragrant with the scent of the great chestnut-tree.*" (*Swann's Way*)

While this dandy and *amateur* of art and good food

introduced the young Proust to Italian art, those closest to him at Illiers or Combray gave him a taste for dishes whose mere mention was enough to make his mouth water.

As early as 1895, in the draft for *Jean Santeuil*, a work which remained unfinished, Proust evoked the power of longing which transforms absence into presence by moulding the very substance of language:

Jean had made this visit so as to find out what they were to have for luncheon, as one who might have hastened there agog for news, news which had nothing Platonic about it and which, though it satisfied his curiosity, caused it to rise at once from its ashes, more sensual, more impatient, than ever for a menu may be as informative as a communiqué, but it is also as exciting as a programme. (...)

"There are baked eggs for lunch today, filet of beef with béarnaise sauce and fried potatoes. Do you like filet béarnaise?" – "I should think I do, Uncle!" – "Good: and there may be gudgeon, too, if old David has brought any – but I can't be sure about that. Good heavens! It's a quarter past eleven, time to be getting home if we don't want the fry to be spoiled!"

(...) Jean with his mind set on baked eggs and filet béarnaise, was beginning to think that the velvety heads of the purple irises on the surface of the water and the fragrant scent of Syrian roses at the corners of the path provided insufficient provender for an appetite sharpened by a morning's work, the passage of time and greed. (Jean Santeuil)

It is undoubtedly in moments such as these, when the recital of menus replaces the act of satisfying the appetite, that one of the great truths of *Remembrance of Things Past* is to be found, namely that it is the experience of longing that is so exquisite and that, in order to create, the artist must cut himself off from the world of the senses and rediscover it from beyond time. The gourmet must combine the poet's eloquence with the artist's eye. In virtually the same terms, Proust describes Jean Santeuil and Oncle Jules practising the delicate alchemic art by which they convert a bowl of cream and a few strawberries into a gastronomic and visual work of art:

After first nibbling a pink biscuit, Jean would crush his strawberries into a portion of cream cheese until the resultant colour gave promise of the taste long dreamed of and now, in a moment or two, to become a reality. Meanwhile, he would add a few more strawberries and a scrap more cream, in carefully calculated proportion, pleasure fighting with concentration in his

eyes, with all the accumulated experience of a colourist and the intuition of an epicure. (Jean Santeuil)

... The cream and the strawberries which this same uncle would mix, always in identical proportions, stopping precisely at the pink colour that he required, with the experience of a colourist and the instinctive foresight of a gourmand. (Preface to Sesame and the Lilies)

This was a feast to delight all the senses, appealing not only to the sense of smell and taste but also to sight – the most "intellectual" sense of all – and sound, with the tinkling of cutlery and crystalware, or the lingering echo of a bell in the noonday heat. Suddenly, the kitchen was no longer a confined space but an entire universe and a work of art whereby each meal became a ceremony in its own right.

Françoise, the cook, presided over this ritual and orchestrated this symphony of the senses.

Who was Françoise? Where did she come from? The unfaltering memory of the young Marcel could have retained the image of more than one of the family's cooks, their faces lit by the glowing heat from the oven, in Auteuil, in Paris and in Illiers. In the same way that every girl in a novel is in fact a synthesis of several girls, it undoubtedly took several of these terrifying and devoted, stern and motherly, kindly and fearful creatures, to create Françoise.

"This early Swann abounding in leisure, fragrant with the scent of the great chestnut-tree, of baskets of raspberries and of a sprig of tarragon."

"All through the month of May the chestnut tree was a mass of blossom. Its innumerable little flowering turrets stood up stiff and close-packed above the spreading calm of leaves looking like a pink forest on the green slope of a mountain." (Overleaf)

"With the hawthorn, white and pink, he associated a memory of the white cream cheese into which, one day, he had crushed his strawberries, so that it flushed with an almost hawthorn colour and remained in recollection as the thing he most liked eating and was for ever begging of the cook..." (Overleaf)

She could have been based on Ernestine Gallou who looked after Proust's paternal grandmother in her tiny converted dwelling above a porchway in the church square in Illiers, until the latter's death in 1889. Or she could have been Félicie Fitau, the Prousts' cook in Paris who made such delicious stewed beef with carrots and who gave her name to the cook in *Jean Santeuil*, where she is described as: *Félicie, like Vulcan at his forge, would be stoking up the fire raking the glowing coals with an iron triangle, in an atmosphere of flame, and heat, and crackling which sounded like the mutterings of Hell. (...) She, whose hands as coarse looking as those of certain sculptors, certain musicians, would be busy composing for him, with an infinity of gentle touches, a wonderfully finished work of art. (Jean Santeuil)*

The subtle recipes created by Françoise were inspired by her own genius or dictated by Tante Léonie who weighed no more than a bunch of cherries and lived on stewed fruit and eggs. The overflowing abundance of the kitchen, that temple of plenty which every day poured its magically renewed contents onto the Proust family's table, seemed to be an attempt to fill a void, the void of Tante Léonie's asceticism. Or so it was in the novel.

Françoise favoured simplicity. In her "little temple of Venus" with its *red-tiled floor gleaming like porphyry. It seemed not so much the cave of Françoise as a little temple of Venus. It would be overflowing with the offerings of the dairyman, the fruiterer, the greengrocer, come sometimes from distant villages to dedicate to the goddess the first-fruits of their fields. And its roof was always crowned with a cooing dove. (Swann's Way)*

She was both goddess and priestess of a brutal cult which fascinated the child:

Françoise, a colonel with all the forces of nature for her subalterns, as in the fairy-tales where giants hire themselves out as scullions, would be stirring the coals, putting the potatoes to steam, and, at the right moment, finishing over the fire those culinary masterpieces which had been first got ready in some of the great array of vessels, triumphs of the potter's craft, which ranged from tubs and boilers and cauldrons and fish kettles down to jars for game, moulds for pastry, and tiny pannikins for cream, through an entire collection of pots and pans of every shape and size. (Swann's Way)

Françoise invested the apparently anarchic profusion of her menus with an order to which she alone held the key. She orchestrated the succession of dishes with a running commentary which justified their existence. She imposed order on the proliferation of produce by controlling it with speech. In that respect, she was on a par with the greatest artists, who transform matter into a work of art:

For upon the permanent foundation of eggs, cutlets, potatoes, preserves, and biscuits, which she no longer even bothered to announce, Françoise would add – as the labour of fields and orchards, the harvest of the tides, the luck of the markets, the kindness of neighbours, and her own genius might provide, so that our bill of fare, like the quatrefoils that were carved on the porches of the cathedrals in the thirteenth century, reflected to some extent the rhythm of the seasons and the incidents of daily life – a brill because the fish-woman had guaranteed its freshness, a turkey because she had seen a beauty in the market at Roussainville-le-Pin, cardoons with marrow because she had never done them for us in that way before, a roast leg of mutton because the fresh air made one hungry and there would be plenty of time for it to "settle down" in the seven hours before dinner, spinach by way of a change, apricots because they were still hard to get, gooseberries because in another fortnight there would be none left, raspberries which M. Swann had brought specially, cherries, the first to come from the cherry-tree which had yielded none for the last two years, a cream cheese, of which in those days I was extremely fond, an almond cake because she had ordered one the evening before, a brioche because it was our turn to make them for the church. And when all this was finished, a

"There may be gudgeon, too, if old David has brought any – but I can't be sure about that."

work composed expressly for ourselves, but dedicated more particularly to my father who had a fondness for such things, a chocolate cream, Françoise's personal inspiration and speciality would be laid before us, light and fleeting as an "occasional" piece of music into which she had poured the whole of her talent. Anyone who refused to partake of it, saying: "No, thank you, I've finished; I'm not hungry any more," would at once have been relegated to the level of those Philistines who, even an artist makes them a present of one of his works, examine its weight and material, whereas what is of value is the creator's intention and his signature. To have left even the tiniest morsel in the dish would have shown as much discourtesy as to rise and leave a concert hall before the end of a piece under the composer's very eyes. (Swann's Way)

Meals became a delightful chronicle of village life and the passing seasons. Once again, Man was living in perfect harmony with nature. Once brought under control, the provisions were painstakingly prepared and transformed into sumptuous still lifes, worthy of the Flemish painters that Proust discovered in the Louvre museum. The cavernous kitchen, glowing red in the light of the constantly burning fire, became a studio where masterpieces were created. Swann was similar to Françoise in that he viewed the humblest of objects and people with an artist's eye. For him, the kitchen maid cleaning asparagus became the figure in a fresco by Giotto:

Poor Giotto's Charity, as Swann had named her, charged by Françoise with the task of preparing them for the table, would have them lying beside her in a basket, while she sat there with a mournful air as though all the sorrows of the world were heaped upon her; and the light crowns of azure which capped the asparagus shoots above their pink jackets were delicately outlined, star by star, as, in Giotto's fresco, are the flowers encircling the brow or patterning the basket of his Virtue at Padua. (Swann's Way)

The smallest object would open up infinite possibilities by combining sophistication with the commonplace, culture with simplicity. Proust painted his own view of the world with an artist's palette and a writer's wit:

I would stop by the table, where the kitchen-maid had shelled them, to inspect the platoons of peas, drawn up in ranks and numbered, like little green marbles, ready for a game;

but what most enraptured me were the asparagus, tinged with ultramarine and pink which shaded off from their heads, finely stippled in mauve and azure, through a series of imperceptible gradations to their white feet — still stained a little by the soil of their garden-bed — with an iridescence that was not of this world. I felt that these celestial hues indicated the presence of exquisite creatures who had been pleased to assume vegetable form and who, through the disguise of their firm, comestible flesh, allowed me to discern in this radiance of earliest dawn, these hinted rainbows, these blue evening shades, that precious quality which I should recognize again when, all night long after a dinner at which I had partaken of them, they played (lyrical and coarse in their jesting as the fairies in Shakespeare's Dream) at transforming my chamber pot into a vase of aromatic perfume. (Swann's Way)

But Françoise also presided over many other mysteries. She was the high priestess of the cruel law of the culinary art which originated in that holy of holies, the scullery: *Françoise had fallen behind. When I went in, I saw her in the scullery which opened on to the back yard, in the process of killing a chicken which, by its desperate and quite natural resistance, accompanied by Françoise, beside herself with rage as she attempted to slit its throat beneath the ear, with shrill cries of "Filthy creature! Filthy creature!," made the saintly meekness and unction of our servant rather less prominent than it would do, next day at dinner, when it made its appearance in a skin gold-embroidered like a chasuble, and its precious juice was poured out drop by drop as from a pyx. When it was dead, Françoise collected its streaming blood, which did not, however, drown her rancour, for she gave vent to another burst of rage, and gazing down at the carcass of her enemy, uttered a final "Filthy creature!" I crept out of the kitchen and upstairs, trembling all over. (Swann's Way)*

The civilized veneer of the recipes exchanged in whispers in the evening or on special occasions had peeled away, revealing a primitive and violent scene which arouses our dormant instincts and in which Françoise represented the darker side of human nature. She did not hesitate to wield a despotic and even sadistic power over her poor defenceless scullery maids. One summer, she served asparagus with surprising persistence: *"Mme Octave, I've got to leave you now; I haven't time to dilly-dally; it's nearly ten o'clock and my fire is not lighted yet, and I've still got to scrape my asparagus."*

"What, Françoise, more asparagus! It's a regular mania for asparagus you've got this year. You'll make our Parisians sick of it."

"No, no, Mme Octave, they like it well enough. They'll be coming back from church soon as hungry as hunters, and they won't turn up their noses at their asparagus." (...) In the year in which we ate such a quantities of asparagus, the kitchen-maid whose duty it was to prepare them was a poor sickly creature, some way "gone" in pregnancy when we arrived at Combray for Easter, and it was indeed surprising that Françoise allowed her to run so many errands and to do so much work. (...) Many years later, we discovered that if we had been fed on asparagus day after day throughout that summer, it was because their smell gave the poor kitchen-maid who had to prepare them such violent attacks of asthma that she was finally obliged to leave my aunt's service. (Swann's Way)

In the scullery at Combray, the young Proust found himself behind the scenes of all artistic creation. By watching Françoise, he came to understand the number of sacrifices required by all works of art. Perhaps it was as he relived this barbaric spectacle that he decided to sacrifice his own life to the *Remembrance of Things Past*.

Françoise drew back the veil which concealed terrifying and cruel mysteries. The young Proust sensed that the culinary art, like the literary art, was violent, and that to check this wave of violence, civilization had introduced a certain number of laws and rituals. The liturgical embellishments which metaphorically surrounded the tender roasted flesh of the dead animal attested to this transition from the wild to the "cultured" state. The pattern of the days was ordered by the unchanging rhythm of meal times, and Tante Léonie's routine was the excessively distorted image of this need for reference points:

In the same way, her love of food was satisfied by the daily, unchanging repetition of a favourite menu; and the anticipation of the same omelette, the same fried potatoes and the same peach compote caused her to conjure up the pleasures to come, hours beforehand. These expectations would have been dashed by the appearance of scrambled eggs, "depriving her of her omelette", or by a portion of cream cheese which, once seen, would have provoked a fresh attack of melancholy, knowing she would not be able to have the compote now until the following day. However, after months of the same

"The back kitchen seemed not so much the cave of Françoise as a little temple of Venus. It would be overflowing with the offerings of the dairyman, the fruiterer, the greengrocer, come sometimes from distant villages to dedicate to the goddess the first-fruits of their fields."

Ernestine Gallou, one of the models for Françoise, in her latter years in Illiers.

"Françoise, a colonel with all the forces of nature for her subalterns, as in the fairytales where giants hire themselves out as scullions, would be stirring the coals, putting the potatoes to steam, and, at the right moment, finishing over the fire those culinary masterpieces which had been first got ready in some of the great array of vessels, triumphs of the potter's craft, which ranged from tubs and boilers and cauldrons and fish kettles down to jars for game, moulds for pastry, and tiny pannikins for cream, through an entire collection of pots and pans of every shape and size."

Joachim Beuckelaer, Kitchen Interior, Musée du Louvre, Paris.

behaviour and identical menus, a penchant for something new would once again emerge and start to gnaw at her. She would say to Françoise: "I must talk to you, I want to change my menu." They would discuss the possibility of boiled eggs. Perhaps as an interim measure, before abandoning the omelette once and for all, she might have one boiled egg and a one-egg omelette, just to see how she got on. (Swann's Way)

A strategy, planned in advance and executed with the precision of a ballet, controlled the smooth running of the operation:

When Jean came in from the paddock just before luncheon, he found the chairs already set about the table. No less punctually than the white noon glare lying still and motionless upon the roads, there, on the table, would be ranged the glittering, motionless, now fully mustered army of the plates with forks and spoons beside them, salt-cellars bringing up the rear, decanters, fewer in number, but taller, each in charge of a rank, and, supreme glory, by every plate a napkin twisted into the shape of a high cap, these being brought on parade by Ernestine only at the last moment, evidence that the hour of noon was close and that when the twelve strokes sounded the guests would wait no longer but take their places, so giving the signal to set in motion all the brilliant array of knives and forks and the procession of dishes which Ernestine, like a preoccupied Commanding Officer, led on, one after the other, a procession to be more than usually enjoyed when a bright sun set the wine in the decanters twinkling and played about the knives and forks. (Jean Santeuil)

Finally, each meal drew to its close with coffee and the mysterious appearance of the scientific instrument entrusted to the care of a serious and thoughtful officiant:

One might include among the simple attributes of agricultural kingship the extremely complicated, because very primitive, piece of machinery which, at this point in the proceedings, the maid set before Monsieur Albert and in which he made the coffee by virtue of a prerogative which he would never have dreamed of sharing with anybody else. If, by chance, he happened to be away, visiting one of his farms, and did not get back for luncheon, "Who'll make the coffee?" became a question of almost national importance. Unless someone of outstanding importance, Monsieur Santeuil, for instance, was on the spot, this task was usually entrusted to the

maid, who was looked upon as a kind of Secretary of State, so that the arbitrary appointment of a substitute was avoided. This machine was made of glass and so contrived that one could see the water coming to the boil, the steam permeating the coffee, and covering the sides of the container with blackish deposit, the water passing through a filter and falling back into a second cylinder from which it was then drawn off. Monsieur Albert listened to the water boiling and that music, though less sophisticated than the military tunes which serve to stimulate more distinguished digestions, but perfectly expressing the sense of well-being of which he was conscious, heralded the coming moment when the bubbling coffee would add to it an exquisite sensation of warmth, sweetness, liveliness and delicate savour and so complete his satisfaction. (Jean Santeuil)

Occasionally, an event occurred which caused an additional ritual to be introduced into a programme which had been definitively established, as was the case on Saturdays at Combray:

Every Saturday, as Françoise had to go in the afternoon to market at Roussainville-le-Pin, the whole household would have to have lunch an hour earlier (...). This acceleration of lunch gave Saturday, for all of us, an individual character, kindly and rather attractive. At the moment when ordinarily there is still an hour to be lived through before the meal-time relaxation, we knew that in a few seconds we should see the arrival of premature endives, a gratuitous omelette, an unmerited beefsteak. (...) Early in the morning, before we were dressed, without rhyme or reason, save for the pleasure of proving the strength of our solidarity, we would call to one another good-humouredly, cordially, patriotically, "Hurry up, there's no time to waste; don't forget it's Saturday!" while my aunt, conferring with Françoise and reflecting that the day would be even longer than usual, would say, "You might cook them a nice bit of veal, seeing that it's Saturday." (Swann's Way)

The family group joined forces to transform this external threat into a secret ritual in which only the initiated participated. An event which could have caused chaos, in fact introduced a mysterious sort of order from which "outsiders" were excluded:

Jokes about Saturday were in fact the only ones we found amusing, because they referred to something peculiar to us and helped to prove how different we were from outsiders (...), that

A COMBRAY MENU

Asparagus

Eggs en cocotte with cream

Fillet of brill

Peas à la française

Individual chocolate creams

Brioche

is, from everyone who dined at the same time on Saturday as they did on every other day. (Swann's Way)

While a degree of latitude was permitted on Saturdays, disrupting the protocol of a dinner party was, on the other hand, tantamount to sacrilege. When Marcel asked Françoise to take a message to his mother who was dining with the only tolerable guest, Charles Swann, his request was met with disapproving silence. Disturb someone at the dining table? Impossible. In spite of this, she complied with his request...

Soon after, she came to tell me that they were only on the salad course and that the butler had not been able to deliver the letter but that as soon as the finger-bowls were passed round, he would slip it to Mamma (...). I opened the window a crack, coffee had been served in the garden and I could hear the buzz of conversation (...). The bells chimed ten o'clock. M. Swann left. I heard Mamma asking my father if he thought the dinner had been enjoyable (...), what he thought of the ice-cream, if M. Swann had helped himself to more chocolate biscuits... (Swann's Way).

Marcel's anguish as he waited for his mother's goodnight kiss was calmed by the names of the various dishes murmured in the gathering darkness. They soothed his childhood desire to devour his mother's cheeks with kisses.

Until the age of ten, Marcel Proust visited Illiers every year. Sometimes, his parents would leave him there to "holiday" alone. Although this was intended to do him good, it in fact plunged him into the "depths of despair" because he was separated from his mother. However, the same doctors who had been recommending that this frail child should have plenty of "fresh air", suddenly forbade these country visits after an initial fit of breathlessness in the Bois de Boulogne made them fear that flowers and trees could precipitate attacks of asthma or hay fever. Marcel only returned to Illiers once more, at the age of fifteen, following the death of his aunt Elisabeth in 1886. It was there, amidst the wonderful enchantment of his books, that he rediscovered the sensual echoes and powerful emotions of his early childhood.

For the first time, he experienced the exquisite bitterness of remembrance. This visit was a prelude to the long years of reclusion in the room at 102,

"Françoise, so active and intelligent, who looked as smart at five o'clock in the morning in her kitchen, under a bonnet whose stiff and dazzling frills seemed to be made of porcelain, as when dressed for high mass." (Opposite)

"... A chocolate cream, light and fleeting as an 'occasional' piece of music..."

boulevard Haussmann, before moving to the sinister room in the rue Hamelin where he was visited by François Mauriac. What Proust's guests did not realize was that they had entered, not just an untidy sick room, but the domain of a gourmet. Their waxen faced host, who used to watch them eat, filled the exercise books cluttering his table with a cuisine of which he alone knew the secret. It was a cuisine which flavoured the regret of what has been "irretrievably lost" with the spicy and subtle taste of happiness regained.

"On the table, would be ranged the glittering, motionless, now fully mustered army of the plates with forks and spoons beside them, salt-cellars bringing up the rear, decanters, fewer in number, but taller, each in charge of a rank, and, supreme glory, by every plate a napkin twisted into the shape of a high cap." (Above)

"The coffee device, tubular and complicated like some piece of physics apparatus that smelt good..." (Opposite)

"We would still be seated in front of our Arabian Nights plates, weighed down by the heat of the day, and even more by our heavy meal." (Overleaf)
Plate No.3 Kalender, a royal prince, part collection, Paris.

THE LADY IN PINK

Alfred Stevens, La Dame en Rose (The Lady in Pink), Musées Royaux des Beaux-Arts, Brussels. (Left)

"A 'newcomer' whom Odette had asked them to invite, (...) the Comte de Forcheville!" (Left)

"The 'winter-garden,' of which in those days the passer-by generally caught a glimpse..." (Opposite)

One of Proust's earliest memories of happiness was playing in the gardens on the Champs-Elysées with Lucie and Antoinette Faure, and especially Marie Benardaky. According to Proust, Marie, although she was never aware of it, was the great love of his life. She was the original model for Gilberte Swann, the daughter of Charles Swann and his wife Odette, a woman of dubious reputation. Indeed, while Marie Benardaky's father was an honorable master of ceremonies at the Tsar's court, her mother was a *demi-mondaine* who was never received in polite society.

Proust says he was thinking of his childhood companion when he described Gilberte's arrival on the Champs-Elysées in the snow. But this was not the narrator's first encounter with this little girl with light auburn hair and flashing black eyes. He had already seen her at Combray, behind that wonderful hawthorn hedge, as he returned from a walk which had taken him in the direction of the Swann's house. On that occasion, she had mesmerized the young boy who was to meet her again in Paris, a meeting which marked Marcel's début in fashionable society. For, although Gilberte fascinated the young man, her mother, Odette, appeared to him as a goddess raised to her elevated position by the sheer determination of her husband, Charles Swann. The only possible explanation for this unsuitable match was an inexplicable and short-lived passion on the part of this refined man for the *demi-mondaine*, Odette de Crécy. But how could the discriminating dandy have allowed himself to be ensnared by the charms of a woman who was definitely not in his class?

Odette had tried to seduce Swann long before Marcel was born. She had invited him to "take tea".

She thought that she showed her originality and expressed her charm when she said to a man, "You'll find me at home any day, fairly late, come to tea."

"And won't you," she had ventured, "come just once and have tea with me?" He had pleaded pressure of work, an essay – which, in reality, he had abandoned years ago – on Vermeer of Delft. "I know that I'm quite useless," she had replied, "a pitiful creature like me beside a learned great man like you. I should be like the frog in the fable! And yet I should so much like to learn, to know things, to be initiated. What fun it would be to become a regular bookworm, to bury my nose in a

lot of old papers!" she had added, with the self-satisfied air which an elegant woman adopts when she insists that her one desire is to undertake, without fear of soiling her fingers, some grubby task, such as cooking the dinner, "really getting down to it herself." (Swann's Way)

However, disdaining the unpleasant realities and violent mysteries of the kitchen, Madame Swann offered her guests dishes of foreign origin whose principle merit as far as she was concerned was that they were fashionable. Perhaps this rejection of the rural tradition represented by Françoise, should be interpreted as an attempt to conceal those very origins which constituted the major obstacle to her social advancement. Family and ancestral tradition was being replaced by snobbery, the consensus of a society which sanctioned certain changing and impermanent values. Odette subscribed to the obsession for all things English which was all the rage at the time. Gilberte was the mirror image of her mother with her ritual of afternoon tea, her mania for introducing English words into the conversation, and her choice of food. Everything bore the mark of this fashion which to the young Marcel seemed the ultimate in elegance:

At half past twelve I would finally make up my mind to enter the house which, like an immense Christmas stocking, seemed ready to bestow upon me supernatural delights. (The French name "Noël" was, by the way, unknown to Mme Swann and Gilberte, who had substituted for it the English "Christmas," and would speak of nothing but "Christmas pudding," what people had given them as "Christmas presents," of going away – the thought of which maddened me with grief – "for Christmas." Even at home I should have thought it degrading to use the word "Noël," and always said "Christmas," which my father considered extremely silly.) (Within a Budding Grove)

The rituals of this society were as complex as the code which governed meals at Combray. Marcel learnt this to his cost at a luncheon given by the Swanns:

At the moment when I was about to step from the hall into the drawing-room, the butler handed me a thin, oblong envelope upon which my name was inscribed. In my surprise I thanked him; but I eyed the envelope with misgivings. I no more knew what I was expected to do with it than a foreigner knows what to do with one of those little utensils that they lay in his place at a Chinese banquet. Noticing that it was gummed down, I was afraid of appearing indiscreet were I to open it then and there, and so I thrust it into my pocket. (...) Meanwhile we had taken our places at table. By the side of my plate I found a carnation, the stalk of which was wrapped in silver paper. It embarrassed me less than the envelope that had been handed to me in the hall, which, however, I had completely forgotten. Its use, strange as it was to me, seemed to me more intelligible when I saw all the male guests take up the similar carnations that were lying by their plates and slip them into their buttonholes. I did as they had done, with the air of naturalness that a free-thinker assumes in church. (...) Another usage, equally strange to me but less ephemeral, disquieted me more. On the other side of my plate was a smaller plate, on which was heaped a blackish substance which I did not then know to be caviare. I was ignorant of what was to be done with it but firmly determined not to let it enter my mouth. (...)

(On his return.) *Leaving my parents, I went upstairs to change my clothes and on emptying my pockets came suddenly upon the envelope which the Swann's butler had handed me before showing me into the drawing-room. I was now alone. I opened it; inside was a card on which was indicated the name of the lady whom I ought to have "taken in" to luncheon.* (Within a Budding Grove)

This initiation into the social graces to some extent sharpened both his powers of observation and his imagination. It was not an entirely futile exercise since a great deal of time was to be spent on futilities before dealing with more important matters. Lunch (Madame Swann used the English word) and dinner marked the stages of social apprenticeship.

However, it was tea and the ritual of taking tea which provided the privileged setting for the awakening of the senses and emotions. These apparently unimportant occasions were pervaded by an atmosphere of solemnity. The conducive half-light of Gilberte's dining room and the boudoir where Odette took tea with Swann created an air of mystery where gourmandise was a sort of communion with the object of desire. The cake offered by Gilberte, which was the focal point of the exchange between the young girl and her passionate young admirer, assumed a mythical dimension which was reinforced by the reference to the

Laure Hayman (1851-1932), photographed by Paul Nadar, 25 November 1879. This *demi-mondaine* and friend of many society men, writers and artists, broke with Proust when she recognized herself in the character of Odette. Proust had to employ all his tact and diplomacy to convince her that she was mistaken. (Above)

Marcel Proust and his childhood companions in the parc Monceau, 1885. Beside him is Lucie Faure, daughter of the future President of France, Félix Faure. (Below)

palace of Darius. These early emotions had something fantastical about them for the young man experiencing them for the first time. He was mesmerized:

The tea-parties (...) to which Gilberte invited her friends, parties which for so long had seemed to me the most insurmountable of the barriers heaped up between her and myself, became now an opportunity for bringing us together (...). Meanwhile, on those tea-party days, pulling myself up the staircase step by step, reason and memory already cast off like outer garments, and myself no more now than the sport of the basest reflexes, I would arrive in the zone in which the scent of Mme Swann greeted my nostrils. I could already visualize the majesty of the chocolate cake, encircled by plates heaped with biscuits, and by tiny napkins of patterned grey damask, as required by convention but peculiar to the Swanns. (...) For when we were all together in Gilberte's little sitting-room, suddenly she would look at the clock and exclaim:

"I say! It's getting a long time since luncheon, and we aren't having dinner till eight. I feel as if I could eat something. What do you say?"

And she would usher us into the dining-room, as sombre as the interior of an Asiatic temple painted by Rembrandt, in which an architectural cake, as urbane and familiar as it was imposing, seemed to be enthroned there on the off-chance as on any other day, in case the fancy seized Gilberte to discrown it of its chocolate battlements and to hew down the steep brown slopes of its ramparts, baked in the oven like the bastions of the palace of Darius. Better still, in proceeding to the demolition of that Ninevite pastry, Gilberte did not consider only her own hunger; she inquired also after mine, while she extracted for me from the crumbling monument a whole glazed slab jewelled with scarlet fruits, in the oriental style. (...) A time would come when I should have to digest the cakes that I took without noticing them. But that time was still remote. Meanwhile Gilberte was making "my" tea. I would go on drinking it indefinitely, although a single cup would keep me awake for twenty-four hours. As a consequence of which my mother used always to say: "What a nuisance it is; this child can never go to the Swanns' without coming home ill." But was I aware even, when I was at the Swann's, that it was tea that I was drinking? (...) Gilberte's girl friends were not all plunged in that state of intoxication. (...) She would nibble away, perched sideways upon a cross-legged seat placed at an angle to the table (...).

Marcel Proust at the age of thirteen, going to a fancy dress party as Little Lord Fauntleroy. (Above)

"She (...) received him in a dressing-gown of mauve crêpe de Chine, drawing its richly embroidered material over her bosom..." (Opposite)

"I say, that looks good, what you've got there. It makes me quite hungry to see you all eating cake." (Overleaf)

Mme Swann, (...) having shown one of her visitors to the door, came sweeping in a moment later, (...) saying with an air of astonishment: "I say, that looks good, what you've got there. It makes me quite hungry to see you all eating cake." (Within a Budding Grove)

Previously, Odette had also received her visitors in an Oriental setting:

(...) A staircase that went straight up between dark painted walls hung with Oriental draperies, strings of Turkish beads, and a huge Japanese lantern suspended by a silken cord (which, however, so that her visitors should not be deprived of the latest comforts of Western civilization, was lighted by a gas-jet inside), to the two drawing-rooms, large and small. These were entered through a narrow vestibule, the wall of which, chequered with the lozenges of a wooden trellis such as you see on garden walls, only gilded, was lined from end to end by a long rectangular box in which bloomed, as in a hothouse, a row of large chrysanthemums, at that time still uncommon though by no means so large as the mammoth specimens which horticulturists have since succeeded in producing. Swann was irritated, as a rule, by the sight of these flowers, which had then been fashionable in Paris for about a year, but it had pleased him, on this occasion, to see the gloom of the vestibule shot with rays of pink and gold and white by the fragrant petals of these ephemeral stars, which kindle their cold fires in the murky atmosphere of winter afternoons. Odette had received him in a pink silk dressing-gown, which left her neck and arms bare. She had made him sit down beside her in one of the many mysterious little alcoves which had been contrived in the various recesses of the room, sheltered by enormous palms growing out of pots of Chinese porcelain, or by screens upon which were fastened photographs and fans and bows of ribbon. (...) She had installed behind his head and beneath his feet great cushions of Japanese silk which she pummelled and buffeted as though to prove that she was prodigal of these riches, regardless of their value. (...) Innumerable lamps burned singly or in pairs upon the different pieces of furniture as upon so many altars, rekindling in the twilight, already almost nocturnal, of this winter afternoon the glow of a sunset more lasting, more roseate, more human... (Swann's Way)

The rooms which provided the setting for these ceremonies of initiation into the art of love were characterized by an almost religious fervour. The "Asiatic temple" with Gilberte's chocolate cake as its centrepiece, and Odette's boudoir lit by lamps placed on the furniture as if on altars, were magical places removed from the world in both time and space. Seduction wove its spell in a subtle complicity between the presence of the woman desired and the satisfaction of desire through food:

Odette poured out Swann's tea, inquired "Lemon or cream?" and, on his answering "Cream, please," said to him with a laugh: "A cloud!" And as he pronounced it excellent, "You see, I know just how you like it." This tea had indeed seemed to Swann, just as it seemed to her, something precious, and love has such a need to find some justification for itself, some guarantee of duration, in pleasures which without it would have no existence and must cease with its passing, that when he left her at seven o'clock to go and dress for the evening, all the way home in his brougham, unable to repress the happiness with which the afternoon's adventure had filled him, he kept repeating to himself: "How nice it would be to have a little woman like that in whose house one could always be certain of finding, what one never can be certain of finding, a really good cup of tea." (Swann's Way)

To this argument in favour of material comfort, Swann added an aesthetic argument. He was struck by Odette's resemblance... *to the figure of Zipporah, Jethro's daughter, which is to be seen in one of the Sistine frescoes. (...) Now that he knew the original in flesh and blood of Jethro's daughter, she became a desire which more than compensated, thenceforward, for the desire which Odette's physical charms had at first failed to inspire in him. When he had sat for a long time gazing at the Botticelli, he would think of his own living Botticelli, who seemed even lovelier still, and as he drew towards him the photograph of Zipporah he would imagine that he was holding Odette against his heart. (Swann's Way)*

The *amateur* of art had become one with the gourmet.

In the vast palette used by Proust to paint *Remembrance of Things Past*, pink was a color particularly associated with Odette. The courtesan used to receive her visitors in the pink light of her boudoir, in a pink silk dressing-gown, surrounded by pink chrysanthemums. Her daughter, Gilberte, appeared from behind a pink and white hawthorn hedge, before the fascinated gaze of the narrator. It was a color already

TEA WITH GILBERTE

Petits fours

Christmas pudding

Fruit cake

Toast

Tea

"And to eradicate even more completely any notion of ceremony, Gilberte would disarrange the chairs that were drawn up round the table, saying, 'It's just like a wedding breakfast. Goodness, how stupid servants are!'"

dear to the young Marcel who associated it with the pink biscuits sold by the grocer in Combray and the color of cream cheese when it was mixed with strawberries. It had subsequently acquired the taste of desire. While mother and daughter played a similar role, the former in the life of Swann, the latter in the life of Marcel, the reader later discovers the virtually unrelated point in common that, unknown to Swann, links him to the young hero. The same Odette de Crécy who had aroused the young man's passion, was also responsible for causing a rift between Marcel's uncle and his family. Once or twice a month, the boy used to go to Paris to visit his Oncle Adolphe (who shared many of the characteristics of Proust's great uncle, Louis Weil) as he was finishing lunch.

At the time, the theatre was a source of great fascination for the nephew in whose eyes the uncle enjoyed the singular distinction (which earned him the general disapproval of the family) of knowing many of the most famous actresses, as well as a great many cocottes, his nephew being unable to distinguish between them. During these visits, his uncle would offer him a piece of marzipan or a tangerine. But following an unannounced visit which, in spite of his promises to his uncle, he lost no time in describing in the most minute detail to his parents, he fell hopelessly in love with the lady in pink whom he had met on that occasion. *On the table was the same plate of biscuits that was always there; my uncle wore the same alpaca coat as on other*

"An architectural cake, as urbane and familiar as it was imposing, seemed to be enthroned there on the off-chance as on any other day, in case the fancy seized Gilberte to discrown it of its chocolate battlements."

days, but opposite him, in a pink silk dress with a great necklace of pearls about her throat, sat a young woman who was just finishing a tangerine. Thus, Odette de Crécy captured the heart of this young innocent who, many years later, was unable to identify Mme Swann with the lady in pink of his childhood.

This intrusion into the world of amorous intrigues was associated with sweetmeats, cakes and pastries. It was an introduction far removed from, and within the context of the novel, completely unrelated to, the lavish tea parties given by Gilberte.

The color pink therefore becomes an indication, which anticipates or acts as a reminder of the pleasures, glimpsed rather than actually experienced, of love. However, the sense of taste remains the most reliable *aide-mémoire*. For example, the taste of *lobster à l'américaine,* reinforced by the bright pink tones associated with this dish, is among the narrator's most vivid memories of his final admittance to the Swanns' circle:

How could I ever dream again of her dining-room as of an inconceivable place, when I could not make the least movement in my mind without crossing the path of that inextinguishable ray cast backwards ad infinitum, into my own most distant past, by the lobster à l'Américaine which I had just been eating. (Within a Budding Grove)

The only dish served by Odette which was not of exotic origin were the creamed eggs which the young guest would savour in advance as he paced up and down in the vicinity of the Swanns' "sanctuary" on the days when his impatience had driven him to arrive much too early for lunch.

I could see from afar in the Swann's little garden-plot the sunlight glittering like hoarfrost from the bare-boughed trees. It is true that the garden boasted only two. (...) These pleasures of nature (intensified by the suppression of habit and indeed by my physical hunger), were infused by the thrilling prospect of sitting down to lunch with Mme Swann. It did not diminish them, (...) it was all as a sort of preface to the creamed eggs, as a patina, a cool pink glaze applied to the decoration of that mystic chapel which was the habitation of Mme Swann, and in the heart of which there was by contrast so much warmth, so many scents and flowers. (Within a Budding Grove)

THE MILITARY PARADISE

"He thought with pleasure of the dinner he was to have when, after walking through Orléans in the dark, he should arrive at last at the café du Loiret and go upstairs to the pleasant little private room with its blazing fire, in which his lieutenant was entertaining."

Marcel Proust in his infantryman's uniform, during his year's voluntary service in the 76th infantry regiment, 1890-1891.

"Moses has put out all
the candles but one
Creating that play of
light and dark
That Daniel Vierge
loved to portray
A candle sprinkled by
the foam
Sprayed from a bottle
of Cliquot
By one of those guests
at the Bon Boeuf
– Pastoral by name, but
less than an inn ..."
Dedication by Proust to
Serge André in a copy
of *Cities of the Plain*.

At the top of the page entitled *Confidences de salon* in Volume XIV of *La revue illustrée*, Proust placed *Marcel Proust par lui-même*. These "confidences" included "the military event that I most admire", which he defined as "My voluntary service!"

It was with this touch of irony that, in 1892, he recalled the very happy memory of his military service completed two years earlier and which he saw as a "paradise". Towards the end of his life, he still thought of it as a time of great friendship and such a strong sense of being useful that he did not want it to end. He enlisted as a "volunteer" after his *baccalauréat*, which meant that he could choose a regiment which was not too far from Paris and that he would be discharged at the end of a year. Marcel Proust served in the 76th infantry regiment at the Coligny barracks in Orléans, from 15 November 1889 to 14 November 1890.

During that year, it was the comradeship that was most important and which gave military life its charm. In spite of his ill health, Proust did not balk at taking part in the demanding physical exercises, nor was this spoilt child excessively repelled by the disorderly confusion of barrackroom life. In December 1889, his mother wrote to him:

"Well, dear, that is one month gone, you only have eleven slices of the cake left to eat, and one or two of those will be eaten while you are on leave.

"I have thought of a way of making the time pass more quickly for you. Buy eleven of your favourite bars of chocolate and tell yourself that you will eat one bar on the last day of each month. You will be surprised how quickly they disappear along with the long months of separation."

The chocolate with its associated taste of childhood was soon replaced by a diet more suited to the appetites of a young man. At the request of his comrades, who were alarmed by his nocturnal bouts of asthma, Proust rented a room in town. His landlady, Mme Ranvoizé, owned a restaurant and rented rooms in her house at 92, faubourg Bannier, near the Coligny barracks. Proust described the house in *Jean Santeuil*:

Each room of the house was occupied by one of Luce's friends, since, as they were all together in the same regiment, they had decided to join forces and have a retreat in the town.

On the ground-floor there was a common dining-room where they foregathered every evening, (...) their occupants had a way of reading their letters and taking their tea with their neighbors. (...) One of them wanted to borrow a sheet of writing-paper from Luce, another to scrounge one of his English biscuits. (Jean Santeuil)

He began to lead a less restricted life where tea was soon replaced by punch:

They (...) arrived at the little house where they had rented a room. They pushed open the door, collected their letters, and went upstairs. Fortunately the room was warm, and Jean asked Madame Ranvoizé to bring up some punch for his friends. "Can you manage that?" – "Sure I can manage it: I'll run round to the grocer for two penn'orth of sugar. I expect there's some rum left. I'd better get a couple of ripe oranges while I'm about it – that all right? There'll be plenty for everyone." (Jean Santeuil)

A period of intense happiness was lit by the flames of this fiery liquid. Far from Paris and the salons, Proust rediscovered within himself the reflections of the stoves presided over by Françoise. He sent home to his surprised parents for vast quantities of wine.

In 1890, his mother devoted an entire section of one of her letters to the "use of wine":

"I have discussed with the wine merchant the best way of sending you the wine. All we are waiting for now is the go-ahead. But your father insists on asking an awkward question:

'What does he want? If he wants it to drink with meals – he would want white wine – but then he couldn't drink Spanish wine with dessert – they don't go together.

'If he only wants Spanish wine, then it is to drink with dessert, but then what does he drink with the main course?'

"This must be resolved before we send anything."
(Correspondance, Vol. I)

The mysterious "use of wine" referred to was possibly its transformation into punch...

The father who had ridiculed the affectation of replacing the French word "Noël" with the English word "Christmas", once again acted as censor and man of good sense. But the young recruit was under the influence of a joyful and boisterous atmosphere in which friendships were formed with alarming ease. Wearing his uniform made Proust feel that he was like the others,

The Coligny barracks, home of the 76th infantry regiment in 1890-1891, in the faubourg Bannier, Orléans.

that he was part of a fraternity, an experience which he found intoxicating:

The door opened and Montargis bounded in. "Ah, how comfortable it is here," I said to him – "You think so?" he asked with a wicked glint in his eye. – "Oh, yes," I answered almost in tears, revelling in this feeling of well-being, alas so short-lived, that had eased my anxiety. – "So you'd rather eat and sleep here with me, than go back to your hotel?" "Oh, Charles, you are cruel," I replied. "It does seem barbaric that it is not allowed, if you knew how wretched I am going to be over there." – "Well, you flatter me, because it occurred to me earlier that you might be happier staying here tonight." And that is precisely what I went to ask the Captain. – "And he agreed," I exclaimed. – "He hadn't the slightest objection. Now, let me get hold of my batman to see to our dinner." An hour later, served by two soldiers, who answered "Yes, Sergeant" every time Charles gave an order and who were so cowed by my presence that they nearly dropped the food on several occasions, we drank Cliquot champagne and ate exquisite partridges, cooked with special care for a friend of the Marquis by the cook. (The Guermantes Way)

The male complicity sanctioned by these libations induced feelings of affection in the hero which his comrades could not understand:

Robert, without being aware of its cause, was touched by my evident affection. This was moreover increased by the sense of well-being inspired in me by the heat of the fire and by the champagne which simultaneously bedewed by forehead with beads of sweat and my eyes with tears; it washed down some young partridges which I ate with the wonderment of a layman of whatever sort he may be, who finds in a way of life with which he is not familiar what he has supposed it to exclude – the wonderment, for instance of an atheist who sits down to an exquisitely cooked dinner in a presbytery. (The Guermantes Way)

The only women who existed in this world were servants whose favours could be bought for a few *louis:*

I thought of Doncières, where every evening I used to meet Robert at his restaurant, and the little dining-rooms there that I had forgotten. I remembered one of these to which I had never given a thought, and which was not in the hotel where Saint-Loup dined but in another, far humbler, a cross between an inn and a boarding-house, where the waiting was done by the landlady and one of her servants. (...) My food was brought to me in a little panelled room upstairs. The lamp went out during dinner and the serving-girl lighted a couple of candles. Pretending that I could not see very well as I held out my plate while she helped me to potatoes, I took her bare fore-arm in my hand, as though to guide her. Seeing that she did not withdraw it, I began to fondle it, then, without saying a word, pulled her towards me, blew out the candles and told her to feel in my pocket for some money. (The Guermantes Way)

A more hearty fare had replaced Odette's ephemeral menus, and the "mesmerized" young admirer had been transformed into a daring and audacious fellow.

Taste was no longer associated with sight but with the sense of touch. We are once again behind the scenes where, against the red glow of kitchen fires, primitive instincts are aroused:

In the courtyard, which opened onto the red glow of the kitchens where chickens were turning on the spit and pigs were roasting, a boy was running carrying a flapping goose by the neck; while the scene that greeted me in the large dining room was reminiscent of some marriage feast at Cana, because of the number of chickens, fish and pheasants which had been brought in, still steaming, by breathless boys and carved immediately on the huge dresser. (The Guermantes Way)

The arousal of desire places the individual in tune with the forces of nature. Eating oysters becomes an act of communion with the marine world:

Right from the oysters, served with Sauterne wines, which usually began dinner and out of whose rough, blackish Gothic shells – lined at the bottom with a thin patina of mother-of-pearl – I sipped several drops of salt water to commune with the living sea, (...) I felt myself fall under the

spell of these intelligent young men who, in their unprecedented kindness, seemed suddenly to have become my friends... (The Guermantes Way)

Amorous adventures with servant girls and rustic feasts blended in a vast canvas worthy of Breugel. The preparations for the secular winter celebrations which gave the café du Loiret the air of a Flemish festival, provided the grand finale to the time at Doncières. But the flames of a forge worthy of Vulcan recalled the glow of Françoise's kitchen and the creative fire of Combray:

At the hotel where I was to meet Saint-Loup and his friends and to which the festive season now beginning attracted a number of people from near and far, I found, as I hurried across the courtyard with its glimpses of glowing kitchens in which chickens were turning on spits, pigs were roasting, lobsters were being flung alive into what the landlord called the "everlasting fire," an influx (worthy of some "Numbering of the People at Bethlehem" such as the Old Flemish masters used to paint) of new arrivals who assembled there in groups, asking the landlord or one of his staff (...) for bed and board, while a scullion hurried past holding a struggling fowl by the neck. (The Guermantes Way)

In this new and Biblical setting, the cook-sculptor, who each day used a red-hot iron to create the ice

"... an influx (worthy of some "Numbering of the People at Bethlehem" such as the Old Flemish masters used to paint) of new arrivals..." Numbering of the People at Bethlehem, Peter Breugel, Musées Royaux des Beaux Arts, Brussels. (Right)

"My affection (...) increased by the sense of well-being inspired by the heat of the fire and by the champagne (...) washed down some partridges which I ate with the wonderment of a layman."

sculptures of animals and human figures on which the desserts would be displayed, became the fiery replica of the Combray Michelangelo. His work was the result of the sudden and paradoxical encounter of fire and ice.

In the courtyard of the hotel in Doncières, the writer was on the verge of making a discovery which would reconcile two principles as contradictory as the solitude of the narrator confronted with the huge dining-room and the incessant movement, the wild exuberance of reality. The "ballet" executed by the servants and the huge piles of food on the tables represented the transient world of the senses, abounding with life. Marcel, initially dazed by the violence of the colors and the noise of the crowd, soon became aware of the aesthetic principle behind the apparent disorder, a principle which was more concerned with creating the impression of a festival atmosphere than satisfying the

diners' appetites. It was a matter of knowing how to create a tableau from the countless pieces of game sacrificed and wasted to this end:

And in the big dining-room which I passed through on the first day before coming to the little room where my friend was waiting for me, it was of some Biblical repast portrayed with medieval naïvety and Flemish exaggeration, that one was reminded by the quantity of fish, chickens, grouse, woodcock, pigeons, brought in dressed and garnished and piping hot by breathless waiters who slid along the polished floor for greater speed and set them down on the huge sideboard where they were carved at once, but where — for many diners were finishing when I arrived — they piled up untouched, as though their profusion and the haste of those who brought them were inspired far less by a desire to meet the requirements of the diners than by respect for the sacred text, scrupulously followed in the letter but naïvely illustrated with real details borrowed

A BACHELOR DINNER

Cancale Oysters

Young partridge in Champagne

Wild duck with cranberries

Chestnut purée

Potatoes baked in woodash

Glacé fruits

Punch

from local custom, and by an aesthetic and religious anxiety to make evident to the eye the splendour of the feast by the profusion of the victuals and assiduity of the servers. One of these stood lost in thought by a sideboard at the far end of the room; and to find out from him, who alone appeared calm enough to be capable of answering me, in which room our table had been laid, I made my way forward among the chafing-dishes that had been lighted here and there to keep the late-comers' plates from growing cold (which did not, however, prevent the dessert, in the centre of the room, from being piled in the outstretched hands of a huge mannikin, sometimes supported on the wings of a duck, apparently of crystal but really of ice, carved afresh every day with a hot iron by a sculptor-cook, quite in the Flemish manner), and, at the risk of being knocked down by his colleagues, went straight towards this servitor in whom I felt I recognized a character traditionally present in these sacred subjects, for he reproduced with scrupulous accuracy the simple, snub-nosed, ill-drawn features and dreamy expression, already half aware of the miracle of a divine presence which the others have not yet begun to suspect. In addition – doubtless in view of the coming festivities – the cast was reinforced by a celestial contingent recruited entirely from a reserve of cherubim and seraphim. A young angel musician, with fair hair framing a fourteen-year-old face, was not, it was true, playing an instrument, but stood musing before a gong or a pile of plates, while other less infantile angels flew swiftly across the boundless expanse of the room, beating the air with the ceaseless fluttering of the napkins which dangled from them like the wings in "primitive" paintings, with pointed ends. Fleeing those ill-defined regions, screened by a hedge of palms, from which the angelic servitors looked, at a distance, as though they had floated down out of the empyrean, I forced my way through to the smaller room in which Saint-Loup's table was laid. (The Guermantes Way)

Doncières was the scene of an amorous discovery too shameful to mention, which belonged to the domain of bachelor suppers and those ambiguous angels carrying food to and from the kitchens. It was also the period during which the writer's temperament was forged in the fire of those briefly glimpsed ovens. Battling with his desires, he advanced, alone, amidst the flames of the plate-warmers, towards a dual mystery whose cruelty he both sensed and feared. To invoke the forbidden delights of these ill-defined regions and contain this vision of the world, he had to make his way, with difficulty, to the safety of a secluded retreat. There he could at last taste those dishes cooked over flames, young partridge flambéd in Champagne, grills and potatoes baked in woodash, not forgetting the lobster flambéd over the "eternal flames", compared with which Mme Swann's *lobster à l'américaine* seemed extremely artificial...

In the course of the gastronomic itinerary of *Remembrance of Things Past*, Doncières was a paradise with a taste of flame, a garden of Eden which was also a den of iniquity.

Between the ages of fifteen and twenty-five, Marcel Proust learnt from the grand masters of the Louvre to "see the world through another's eyes". Chardin was responsible for his discovery of "the hidden life of still lifes" and the beauty of everyday meals:

"On that sideboard where, from the hurried folds in the half turned-back cloth to the knife set sideways, its whole handle protuding, everything preserves the memory of the servants' haste, everything bespeaks the gluttony of the guests. The fruit-bowl, as glorious still though now plundered as an orchard in autumn, is topped off by peaches as pink and chubby as cherubims, as sunny and inaccessible as immortals. A dog cranes its head but cannot reach up to them and makes them the more desirable for being truly desired." Jean-Baptiste Chardin, le Buffet, Musée du Louvre, Paris.

WEDNESDAYS WITH MADAME VERDURIN

Illustration by Madeleine Lemaire for "A Dinner in Town", from the collection of essays *Pleasures and Regrets*, published in 1896. Proust is sitting in the centre, facing us. (Above)

Madame Verdurin did not give "dinners", but she had "Wednesdays". Her Wednesdays were works of art...

"The mistress of the house, who has placed me next to her at dinner, graciously tells me before we go in that she has flowered her table with nothing but Japanese chrysanthemums – but chrysanthemums displayed in vases which are the rarest masterpieces, one in particular of bronze on which petals of red-gold copper seem to have been shed by the living flower."

In his descriptions of the exclusive Verdurin set, Marcel Proust depicted another of the social types encountered in the society world he had frequented as a young man. The society hostesses were the first to introduce him into certain social circles and were to some extent responsible for launching "the young Proust". With their loyal following of artists and scholars, these women reigned over the artistic and literary world of Paris, "made" members of the French Academy, promoted Wagner and "modern" art, had their own particular "day" and equated the luxury of their dinner parties with the reputation of their salon. In 1896, this agreeable and cultured young man who loved literature, published – albeit with great difficulty – his first work, *Les plaisirs et les jours, (Pleasures and Regrets)* originally to have been entitled "Le Château de Réveillon". This collection of short texts, presented in an elaborately ornate volume, with a preface by Anatole France and water color illustrations by Madeleine Lemaire, was considered to be superficial by some of the few who read it. The work earned Proust a reputation for conceitedness and social snobbery.

Because they were associated with the first amorous intrigue of the novel, namely between Swann and Odette, as well as the literary apprenticeship of the hero, the Verdurins occupied a strategically important place in *Remembrance of Things Past*. The story of the characters' romantic involvement and the artistic destiny of their creator unfolds in a decor of exquisitely decorated tables and lavishly prepared meals.

The Verdurins never invited you to dinner; you had your "place laid" there. There was never any programme for the evening's entertainment. The young pianist would play, but only if "the spirit moved him," for no one was forced to do anything, and, as M. Verdurin used to say: "We're all friends here. Liberty Hall, you know!" (...)

Evening dress was barred, because you were all "good pals" and didn't want to look like the "boring people" who were to be avoided like the plague and only asked to the big evenings, which were given as seldom as possible and then only if it would amuse the painter or make the musician better known. The rest of the time you were quite happy playing charades and having supper in fancy dress, and there was no need to mingle any alien ingredient with the little "clan". (Swann's Way)

Whereas Odette, who was to become Mme Swann, was fascinated by all things English, the Verdurin set shared the general enthusiasm for "Japonisme".

Far Eastern art had been made fashionable by such critics as the de Goncourt brothers and exhibitions at the Ecole des Beaux-Arts, and was in fact all the rage at the time that *Swann in Love* was set. At the dinner party where Swann was among the guests, the Japanese salad referred to by Alexandre Dumas (fils) was one of the topics of conversation:

Mme Cottard, who was a modest woman and spoke but seldom, was not however lacking in self-assurance when a happy inspiration put the right word in her mouth. She felt that it would be well received, and this gave her confidence, but what she did with it was with the object not so much of shining herself as of helping her husband on in his career. And so she did not allow the word "salad," which Mme Verdurin had just uttered, to pass unchallenged.

"It's not a Japanese salad, is it?" she said in a loud undertone, turning towards Odette.

And then, in her joy and confusion at the aptness and daring of making so discreet and yet so unmistakable an allusion to the new and brilliantly successful play by Dumas, she broke into a charming, girlish laugh, not very loud, but so irresistible that it was some time before she could control it.

"Who is that lady? She seems devilish clever," said Forcheville.

"No, it is not. But we'll make one for you if you'll come to dinner on Friday."

"You will think me dreadfully provincial," said Mme Cottard to Swann, "but I haven't yet seen this famous Francillon that everybody's talking about. (...) I must confess I didn't think it very sensible for him to spend money on seats in order to see it again with me. Of course an evening at the Théâtre-Français is never really wasted; the acting's good there always; but we have some very nice friends' (Mme Cottard rarely uttered a proper name, but restricted herself to "some friends of ours" or "one of my friends," as being more "distinguished," speaking in an affected tone and with the self-importance of a person who need give names only when she chooses) 'who often have a box, and are kind enough to take us to all the new pieces that are worth going to, and so I'm certain to see Francillon sooner or later, and then I shall know what to

think. But I do feel such a fool about it, I must confess, for wherever I go I naturally find everybody talking about that wretched Japanese salad. In fact one's beginning to get just a little tired of hearing about it," she went on, seeing that Swann seemed less interested than she had hoped in so burning a topic. "I must admit, though, that it provides an excuse for some quite amusing notions. I've got a friend, now, who is most oroginal, though she's a very pretty woman, very popular in society, very sought-after, and she tells me that she got her cook to make one of these Japanese salads, putting in everything that young M. Dumas says you're to in the play. Then she asked a few friends to come and taste it. I was not among the favoured few, I'm sorry to say. But she told us all about it at her next "at home"; it seems it was quite horrible, he made us all laugh till we cried. But of course it's all in the telling," Mme added, seeing that Swann still looked grave.

And imagining that it was perhaps because he had not liked Francillon: "Well, I daresay I shall be disappointed with it after all. I don't suppose it's as good as the piece Mme de Crécy worships, Serge Panine. There's a play, if you like; really deep, makes you think! But just fancy giving a recipe for a salad on the stage of the Théâtre Français!" (Swann's Way)

Swann remained unmoved by the reference to the Japanese salad. He was mesmerized by Odette whom he was seeing for the first time in this would-be "artistic" circle.

The "artistic genre" had been introduced by the de Goncourt brothers and had flourished in the confused muddle of their "garret" in Auteuil. This had been the meeting place for their literary friends who would later define and appreciate art in the manner of true connoisseurs. The next generation met in Madeleine Lemaire's studio, in her tiny house in the rue de Monceau, which provided the crowded venue for the "camarades", the big names in the art world and the aristocracy who came to rub shoulders with the rank and file. This was where Proust "sketched" his "genre paintings" of the Verdurin set. Swann, who is an echo of Proust in this social milieu, questions one of the guests, an artist:

The latter, it appeared, had been that afternoon to an exhibition of the work of another artist, also a friend of Mme Verdurin, who had recently died, and Swann wished to find

out from him (for he valued his discrimination) whether there had really been anything more in these last works than the virtuosity which had struck people so forcibly in his earlier exhibitions.

"From that point of view it was remarkable, but it did not seem to me to be a form of art which you could call 'elevated'," said Swann with a smile.

"Elevated ... to the purple," interrupted Cottard, raising his arms with mock solelmnity. The whole table burst out laughing.

"What did I tell you?" said Mme Verdurin to Forcheville. "It's simply impossible to be serious with him. When you least expect it, out he comes with some piece of foolery."

But she observed that Swann alone had not unbent. For one thing he was none too pleased with Cottard or having secured a laugh at his expense in ront of Forcheville. But the painter, instead of replying in a way that might have interested Swann, as he would probably have done had they

Henri:

I should be most happy, Miss Annette, to have the recipe of the salad that we have eaten at dinner here. I was told it was of your compounding.

Annette:

The Japanese salad.

Henri:

Is it Japanese?

Annette:

I call it so.

Henri:

Why?

Annette:

To give it a name. Everything is Japanese nowadays.

Henri:

Are you the inventor of it?

Annette:

Certainly. I am extremely fond of cooking.

Alexandre Dumas fils, Francillon, Act I, Scene II, 1887.

DINNER WITH MADAME VERDURIN

Salade "Francillon"

Grilled Crawfish

Sole à la normande

Salad

Strawberry mousse

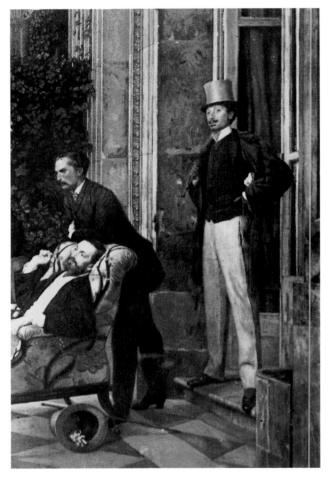

"And yet, my dear Charles Swann, (...) If, in Tissot's picture representing the balcony of the Rue Royale club, where you figure with Galliffet, Edmond de Polignac and Saint-Maurice, people are always drawing attention to you, it is because they know that there are some traces of you in the character of Swann."
James Tissot, le Balcon du Cercle de la rue Royale, 1868. Detail: Charles Haas, the original model for Swann.

been alone together, preferred to win the easy admiration of the rest with a witty dissertation on the talent of the deceased master.

"I went up to one of them," he began, "just to see how it was done. I stuck my nose into it. Well, it's just not true! Impossible to say whether it was done with glue, with soap, with sealing-wax, with sunshine, with leaven, with caca!"

"And one makes twelve!" shouted the doctor, but just too late, for no one saw the point of his interruption.

"It looks as though it was done with nothing at all," resumed the painter. "No more chance of discovering the trick than there is in the 'Night Watch' or the 'Female Regents,' and technically it's even better then Rembrandt or Hals. It's all there but really, I swear it.' (...) (Swann's Way)

"It smells good, it makes your head whirl; it takes your breath away; you feel ticklish all over – and not the faintest clue to how it's done. The man's a sorcerer; the thing's a conjuring-trick, a miracle," bursting into outright laughter, "it's almost dishonest!" And stopping, solemnly raising his head, pitching his voice on a basso profundo note which he struggled to bring into harmony, he concluded, "And it's so sincere!"

Except at the moment when he had called it "better than the 'Night Watch,'" a blasphemy which had called forth an instant protest from Mme Verdurin, who regarded the "Night Watch" as the supreme masterpiece of the universe (conjointly with the "Ninth" and the "Winged Victory"), and at the word "caca," which had made Forcheville throw a sweeping glance round the table to see whether it was "all right," before he allowed his lips to curve in a prudish and conciliatory smile, all the guests (save Swann) had kept their fascinated and adoring eyes fixed upon the painter. (Swann's Way)

Swann's attitude was disastrous. It ran the risk of losing him the friendship of the *Patronne*, who did not suffer bores gladly. The only Jewish member of the Jockey Club was to have great difficulty in winning the approval of the Verdurin set.

But surely Swann, like Proust himself, was the only person to view this social milieu with a critical eye. According to Edmond de Goncourt, it was a milieu in which these "artistic souls" appeared ridiculous because they took themselves so seriously – even when making a joke – that they tended to ignore the value of true art. And so it was that as they listened to the painter, the guests paid scant attention to what they were eating:

"No, really, I'm not joking!" protested the painter, *enchanted by the success of his speech. "You all look as if you thought I was pulling your legs, that it's all eyewash. I'll take you to see the show, and then you can say whether I've been exaggerating; I'll bet you anything you like, you'll come away even more enthusiastic than I am!"*

"But we don't suppose for a moment that you're exaggerating. We only want you to go on with your dinner, and my husband too. Give M. Biche some more sole, can't you see his has got cold? We're not in any hurry; you're dashing round as if the house was on fire. Wait a little; don't serve the salad just yet." (Swann's Way)

Mme Verdurin represented the voice of reason with her *sole à la normande*, a reliable feature of nineteenth-century cuisine, which combined provincial flavour with gastronomic tradition. The *salade Francillon* might constitute a new attraction for some future dinner party but could not compete with recipes which were tried and tested. She asserted her "artistic soul" by her attachment to the beauties of the past:

Odette had gone to sit on a tapestry-covered settee near the piano. (...) "What charming Beauvais!" said Swann politely, (...) "Ah! I'm glad you appreciate my settee," replied Mme Verdurin, "and I warn you that if you expect ever to see another like it you may as well abandon the idea at once. They've never made anything else like it. (...) Just look at the little friezes round the edges; here, look, the little vine on a red background in this one, the Bear and the Grapes. Isn't it well drawn? What do you say? I think they knew a thing or two about drawing! Doesn't it make your mouth water, that vine? My husband makes out that I'm not fond of fruit, because I eat less of them than he does. But not a bit of it, I'm greedier than any of you, but I have no need to fill my mouth with them when I can feed on them with my eyes. What are you all laughing at now, pray? Ask the doctor; he'll tell you that those grapes act on me like a regular purge. Some people go to Fontainebleau for cures; I take my own little Beauvais cure here." (Swann's Way)

Most probably because of a hypersensitive disposition which caused her to suffer "continual migraines" when listening to Wagner and to – literally – dislocate her jaw while laughing, Mme Verdurin found it more elegant to indulge in the simple contemplation of an objet d'art, than in the consumption of more earthly nourishment. She fed her guests, but reserved herself the spiritual pleasure of "feasting her eyes".

The Verdurin milieu was a pastiche of the "artistic milieu". It was a literary genre in which Marcel Proust excelled in the early stages of his literary career. In *Time Regained*, the final part of *Remembrance of Things Past,* he incorporated into his own writing a *trompe-l'oeil* effect in the form of an imaginary extract from an actual publication, the *Journal* edited by the de Goncourt brothers. In this extract, Proust imagined that Edmond de Goncourt was giving an account of one of the Verdurins' dinner parties. These imaginary pages, intended to serve as a real warning to people who were equally fictitious, were written in the "artistic style" which had become fashionable as a result of the essay on the wood block print artist, Hokusai, published by Edmond de Goncourt in 1896:

"And the care devoted to the choice of these combs! With here, a scattering of flower petals, and there a swathe of irises, and garlands of morning glory, and over there the crowning glory of a single water lily. Not to mention cranes in full flight, clouds of mandarin ducks, and flocks of starlings..." (Edmond de Goncourt, Hokusai)

In producing this pastiche, Proust stressed the artificiality of the Verdurins' table, since the long list of decorative details obscures what should be the true substance of the dinner party, namely the courses served.

On the infrequent occasions when the contents of the dishes are mentioned, they are described with a simplicity which is in fact an additional subtlety, since they are totally eclipsed by the invasive decor:

The mistress of the house, who has placed me next to her at dinner, graciously tells me before we go in that she flowered her table with nothing but Japanese chrysanthemums – but chrysanthemums displayed in vases which are the rarest masterpieces, one in particular of bronze on which petals of red-gold copper seem to have been shed by the living flower. Cottard, the doctor, is there, his wife, the Polish sculptor Viradobetski, Swann the collector, and an aristocratic Russian lady, a princess with a name ending in -off which I fail to catch. (...) We go in to dinner, and there follows an extraordinary cavalcade of plates which are nothing less than

masterpieces of the porcelainist's art, that artist whose chatter, during an exquisite meal, is heard with more pleasure than any fellow guest's by the titillated attention of the connoisseur – Yung Cheng plates with nasturtium-colored borders and purple-blue irises, leafless and tumid, and those supremely decorative flights of kingfishers and cranes trailing across a dawn sky, a dawn that has just the early-morning tones glimpsed daily from Boulevard Montorency by my awakening eyes – Dresden plates daintier and of more graceful workmanship, with drowsy, bloodless roses fading into violet, with ragged-edged tulips the color of wine-lees, with the rococo elegance of a pink or a forget-me-not – Sèvres plates meshed with the close guilloche of their white fluting, whorled in gold, or knotted with a golden ribbon that stands in gallant relief upon the creamy smoothness of the paste – finally a whole service of silver plate arabesqued with those myrtles of Luciennes that were not unknown to the Dubarry. And what is perhaps equally rare is the truly quite remarkable quality of the things served upon these plates, a meal most subtly concocted, a real spread such as Parisians, one cannot say it too emphatically, never have at their really grand dinner parties and which reminds me of certain prize dishes of Jean d'Heurs. Even the foie gras bears no resemblance to the insipid mousse customarily served under that name; and I do not know many places in which a simple potato salad is made as it is here with potatoes firm as Japanese ivory buttons and patina'd like those little ivory spoons with which Chinese women sprinkle water over their new-caught fish. Into the Venetian glass which I have before me is poured, like a rich cascade of red jewels, an extraordinary Léoville bought at M. Montalivet's sale, and it is a delight to the imagination of the eye and also, I am not afraid to say it, of what used to be called the gullet, to see a brill placed before us which has nothing in common with those anything but fresh brills that are served at the most luxurious tables, which in the slow course of their journey from the sea have had the pattern of their bones imprinted upon their backs; a brill that is served not with the sticky paste prepared under the name of white sauce by so many chefs in great houses, but with a genuine white sauce, made with butter that costs five francs a pound; to see this brill brought in on a wonderful Ching Hon dish streaked with the purple rays of a sun setting above a sea upon which ludicrously sails a flotilla of large lobsters, their spiky stippling rendered with such extraordinary skill that they seem

"Jean could see the dining-room brilliantly illuminated under the lamp, his friends assembled, dinner on the table, and a letter waiting for him under his white napkin."

to have been moulded from living shells, with a border too depicting a little Chinaman who plays with rod and line a fish whose silver and azure belly makes it a marvel of iridescent color. (*Time Regained*)

Whereas Mme Verdurin delighted in artificiality, her husband had not lost his taste for the simple things in life. With a sigh, his wife confided in one of her guests, Edmond de Goncourt:

When I remark to Verdurin what an exquisite pleasure it must be for him to eat this rare and subtle grub off a collection such as no prince today possesses in his show cases: "It is easy to see that you don't know him," gloomily interjects the mistress of the house. And she speaks to me of her husband as of an original and a crank, indifferent to all these dainties, "a crank," she repeats, "yes, that is the only word for it, a crank who would get more enjoyment from a bottle of cider drunk in the somewhat plebeian coolness of a Normandy farm." (*Time Regained*)

According to Mme Verdurin, Normandy was like the grounds of an English country house, while her guest went even further in this "poeticized" evocation of a province where peasants' cottages were adorned with a shower of sulphur-yellow roses, where two intertwined pear trees looked like an ornamental inn sign, and where you could walk in real forests whose blossoms were like swathes of pink tulle.

However, at la Raspelière, the property in Normandy rented every year by the Verdurins, it was the Patron who was the host:

We had turned into the drive of la Raspelière where M. Verdurin stood waiting for us on the steps. "I did well to put on a dinner-jacket," he said, observing with pleasure that the faithful had put on theirs, "since I have such smart gentlemen in my party."

Come along, my dear Brichot, get your things off quickly. We have a bouillabaisse which mustn't be kept waiting." "What, are you still talking about Dechambre?" said M. Verdurin, who had gone on ahead of us (...) "Listen," he said to Brichot, "don't let's exaggerate. The fact of his being dead is no excuse for making him out a genius, which he was not. He played well, I admit, but the main thing was that he was in the right surroundings here; transplanted, he ceased to exist. My wife was infatuated with him and made his reputation. You know what she's like. I will go further: in the

interest of his own reputation he died at the right moment, à point, as the lobsters, grilled according to Pampille's incomparable recipe, are going to be, I hope (unless you keep us standing here all night with your jeremiads in this kasbah exposed to all the winds of heaven)." (*Cities of the Plain*)

When Marcel was invited to this country retreat, he found that his hosts' basic attitude towards matters related to the culinary art was more easily understood than in Paris. One of the guests, a distinguished Norwegian philosopher, irritated the Patronne by asking questions which delayed the progress of her dinner:

"But I must point out to Madame that if I have permitted myself this questionnaire – pardon me, this questation – it is because I have to return tomorrow to Paris to dine at the Tour d'Argent or at the Hôtel Meurice.

"The Tour d'Argent is not nearly as good as they make out," said Mme Verdurin, sourly. "In fact, I've had some disgusting dinners there."

"But am I mistaken, is not the food one consumes at Madame's table an example of the finest French cookery?"

"Well, it's not positively bad," replied Mme Verdurin, mollified. "And if you come next Wednesday, it will be better." (*Cities of the Plain*)

If Mme Verdurin was extremely sensitive about the reputation of her dinner parties and served her guests food which had been carefully and lovingly prepared, it was more through social vanity than personal taste. Although the food she served was excellent, it was served with the sole intention of having it praised in other houses, in the presence of other hostesses whose jealousy she wanted to arouse. The ostentation of her dinner services was entirely in keeping with this desire to outshine others, at whatever cost, in the competitive milieu of Paris. Courses were not chosen on their culinary merits, but always in terms of the effect they would produce:

"What is this prettily colored thing that we're eating?" asked Ski.

"It's called strawberry mousse," said Mme Verdurin.

"But it's ex-qui-site. You ought to open bottles of Château-Margaux, Château-Lafite, port wine."

"I can't tell you how he amuses me, he never drinks anything but water," said Mme Verdurin, seeking to cloak

"As the result of a knuckle of ham, a pâté, a strawberry mousse – which gave to the Santeuil table an appearance of unusual richness." (Above)

"She had not ordered all the fruit from the same place, but the grapes from Crapote, whose speciality they were, the strawberries from Jauret, the pears from Chevet, who always had the best, and so on." (Opposite)

with her delight at this flight of fancy her alarm at the thought of such extravagance.

"But not to drink," Ski went on. "You shall fill all our glasses, and they will bring in marvellous peaches, huge nectarines; there, against the sunset, it will be as luscious as a beautiful Veronese."

"It would cost almost as much," M. Verdurin murmured.

"But take away those cheeses with their hideous color," said Ski, trying to snatch the plate from in front of his host, who defended his gruyère with all his might. (Cities of the Plain)

Only the Patron "defending his gruyère", was not seduced by the aesthetic visions of his so-called "artistic" guests. He preferred a piece of cheese to the enraptured contemplation of a still life of red fruit against a background of the setting sun. In the midst of these socialites who were continually inverting values and confusing originality with authenticity, he retained the rustic good sense that gave him his taste for cider and made him choose food of the very highest quality which satisfied what used to be referred to as the "appetite" rather than the imagination.

In *Remembrance of Things Past*, Proust saw the provinces not so much as a contrast, but rather as a complement to and extension of the splendours of Parisian society. They provided the etymological origins of his work. The oldest families in France, whose names fire the imagination, could trace their origins to the provinces. And it was there that one still encountered such admirable men as the doyen de Doville, the possessor of a true knowledge (which remained incomprehensible to ears too accustomed to the general hubbub of Parisian dinner parties), who was capable of delighting his guests with that extremely simple dish which is so very difficult to prepare successfully: fried potatoes.

I asked Brichot if he knew what the word Balbec meant. "Balbec is probably a corruption of Dalbec," he told me. "One would have to consult the charters of the Kings of England, (...) So it was explained to me by the incumbent of Douville, a bald, eloquent, fanciful man and a devotee of the table, who lives by the rule of Brillat-Savarin, and who expounded to me in somewhat sibylline terms a loose pedagogy, while he fed me upon some admirable fried potatoes. (Cities of the Plain)

IN HIGH SOCIETY

The comtesse Henri Greffulhe, née Elisabeth de Caraman-Chimay (1860-1952), one of Proust's models for the duchesse de Guermantes. This photograph was taken by Paul Nadar on 30 May 1895. (Above)

"At each of the four corners of the table bunches of blue-green maidenhair fern, and in the middle zinnias, red, yellow and mauve, snapdragons and African marigolds, gathered by Mlle de Réveillon in the course of her morning walk in the Park, all freshly plucked, showed the full brightness of their tints (...) and caught the gay beams of sunlight which had pursued them into the confines of the room, imparting to them that especial subtlety of tone..." (Opposite)

Although Réveillon and Guermantes, both in Seine-et-Marne, are only a few miles apart, in real life Marcel Proust never travelled from one to the other. He did stay at Réveillon, with his friend Reynaldo Hahn, for a few days in the autumn of 1895, but Guermantes belongs to the purely imaginary realm, associated in the mind of his hero – like the duke and duchess themselves – with the mystery of the Merovingian past, bathed, as if by a sunset, in the orangey light emanating from the syllable "antes".

Like his hero, Marcel Proust could say: "Never on our walks in the Guermantes direction did we push on as far as my desired goal and reach Guermantes itself."

In 1895, the Château de Réveillon was owned by the well-known flower painter Madeleine Lemaire, to whom Proust wrote: "You outdo God, making it spring all the year round." In *Jean Santeuil*, Réveillon is a place of sophisticated rustic pleasures, where the hero is the guest of the duke and duchess de Réveillon and their son Henry, his friend.

The other members of the family were only just going into the dining-room. At each of the four corners of the table bunches of blue-green maidenhair fern, and in the middle zinnias, red, yellow and mauve, snapdragons and African marigolds, gathered by Mlle de Réveillon in the course of her morning walk in the Park, all freshly plucked, showed the full brightness of their tints on which lay a patina of dew as yet not dried, and caught the gay beams of sunlight which, from the depths of the Park, had pursued them into the confines of the room, imparting to them that especial subtlety of tone which made them look like painted flowers upon the surface of the porcelain stands in which they were arranged, carnations stiff and upright, or violets blooming on their green and rounded stalks, so that reflected on the white-panelled walls, they produced the impression of motionless designs, as blue as hyacinths, as red as roses. But already eggs were steaming between the fresh tints of the flowers. Chairs were pulled to the table, napkins spread on waiting knees, napkins as fresh and innocent as the joy sparkling in every eye and now enhanced by the discovery, between the golden waves of scrambled eggs, of little fleets of bacon, half drowned and barely visible, which those, now seated, began with a will to rescue from the wreck. This, to be accurate, was no surprise to the duchesse de Réveillon who that very morning had conceived the idea and

When Proust stayed there, the Château de Réveillon was owned by Madeleine Lemaire, who tended a model rose garden and kept a magnificent troupe of peacocks.
This photograph of Madeleine Lemaire (1845-1928), née Jeanne-Magdeleine Coll, was taken by Paul Nadar in 1891.

"The Réveillon family mansion, one of those rare aristocratic establishments which has not become just another example of the houses I have described, in other words, "smart" and utterly devoid of personality. (...) It came as a surprise to Hénri de Réveillon that every wallpaper, every picture, every comfit-box might have something to tell him, though scrappy and vague perhaps, and that the smooth running commentary with which their exhibiting was accompanied, seemed to tell him more about the arts than he had ever thought there was to know."

imparted it to the cook. But, though the pleasure of discovery was not for her, and perhaps because consciousness of success brought its own satisfaction, she seemed to be far from displeased. The author of a successful play cannot share the thrill of gratified curiosity which the audience feels, being still ignorant of what is to happen on the stage. But applause gives him a different variant of delight which is not to be despised. The duke and Henri mingled their pleasure with Jean's. This was not for them, as it was for him, the first time that they had eaten scrambled eggs and bacon. But the joys of habit are often more to be relished than those of novelty. A dish of hot lobster, set in readiness for Mlle de Réveillon who never ate eggs, added to the pleasing smell of zinnias and snapdragon a fragrance which was not, as was theirs, an end in itself, but was destined to add the finishing touch to an anticipated, and more material, form of possession. (Jean Santeuil)

Even during the winter months, however,

...the duchess disliked entertaining on a grand scale at Réveillon, she equally disliked being there alone. Consequently, friends were for ever turning up to stay for a few days (...). Letters were written calling the faithful to the colors. "The blue room is waiting for you. Boniface has now got a range on which he can concoct lièvre à l'allemande just as you like it. (...) In October when the weather was fine, one took a walk before dinner as in summer, about seven o'clock. (...) There was something exciting, stimulating, in starting off like that before dinner when it was already dark, and prolonging the walk before returning to dine, in the full light of the moon and under the stars through a sleeping countryside, in a silence so completely hedging one in (...). But it was lovely all the same just when one was beginning to feel cold and hungry, to return through the village and to see between the trees of the Park light streaming from the windows of the drawing-room and dining-room, and to imagine in anticipation what was already there awaiting one's arrival, though one would not actually see it for several more minutes — the glow of the fire, (...) under the lamp, the hot soup in one's plate. (Jean Santeuil)

In *Remembrance of Things Past*, the hero can only dream of life in a big country house:

All day long, during these walks, I had been able to muse upon the pleasure of being the friend of the duchesse de Guermantes, of fishing for trout, of drifting in a boat on the

Vivonne; and, greedy for happiness, I asked nothing more from life in such moments than that it should consist always of a series of joyous afternoons. (Swann's Way)

Later, he does become acquainted with the duke and duchess, but in Paris – his family having by chance moved in to the neighboring apartment:

In the house in which we had now come to live, the great lady at the end of the courtyard was a duchess, elegant and still young. She was, in fact, Mme de Guermantes and, thanks to Françoise, I soon came to know all about her household. For the Guermantes (to whom Françoise regularly alluded as the people "below," or "downstairs") were her constant preoccupation from first thing in the morning when, as she did Mamma's hair, casting a forbidden, irresistible, furtive glance down into the courtyard, she would say: (...) "Oh! Just look at the fine pheasants in the kitchen window. No need to ask where they've become from: the duke's been out with his gun!" (The Guermantes Way)

The Guermantes always have something of the country about them, sweet-smelling and wholesome, stemming from an aristocratic attachment to their ancestral lands. For the narrator, since childhood, Oriane de Guermantes had the aura of a character from a magic lantern show; now, the duke and duchess seem like figures in an antique tapestry, set against a background of woodland abounding in game. On their Paris apartment, as once on Françoise's kitchen at Combray, converge offerings from their country estates.

No room here for the artistic affectation of the Verdurins. A love of good things makes the Guermantes' dining-room, though cultured, a place of real pleasure in eating and of simple tastes:

M. and Mme de Guermantes, who were extremely fond of good food and whose fare was delicious, believed that throwing exquisite dinners, if only for one or two people, was a sort of duty which they were delighted to carry out several times each week lavishly, formally and without affectation. This meal, moreover, like the meal eaten by the first Christians, was a sort of mystic and social communion.

Along with a young partridge prepared according to rare recipes known by M. Guermantes, they served up their acquaintances, such as their old friend, the duc d'Albon, their niece, Her Highness, the princesse de Weinbourg, when she was visiting, M. Bréfort, unfortunately! and many others. These

Jean Béraud, la Réception, Private collection, Paris.

introductions, made in such a way that all the guests centred their attention on me when they arrived, the familiar talk shared during the meal by these smartly dressed people, the hosts, also, so elegant, but also so forthright and cheerful, were, for M. and Mme de Guermantes, pleasures equal to relishing the partridges and savouring the Château d'Yquem. (The Guermantes Way)

Oriane de Guermantes loathes all those things which, to Mme Verdurin, appear "distinguished" and "original". In her conversation, she *rejects everything to do with fine language and the expression of lofty thoughts, so that she made it a sort of point of good breeding when she was with a poet or a musician to talk only of the food that they were eating or the game of cards to which they would afterwards sit down. (The Guermantes Way)*

For Marcel Proust, the down-to-earth tenor of her conversation – not uncommon in her social circles – has something disturbing or even mysterious about it. Invited to dinner together with some famous poet, and consumed with curiosity as to what they will discuss, a guest may be suprised to hear the duchess talk to him about the weather:

They would sit down to lunch. "Do you like this way of doing eggs?" she would ask the poet. On hearing his approval, which she shared, for everything in her own house appeared to her exquisite, down to a horrible cider which she imported from Guermantes: "Give Monsieur some more eggs," she would tell the butler, while the anxious fellow guest sat waiting for what must surely have been the object of the occasion, since they had arranged to meet, in spite of every sort of difficulty, before the duchess, the poet and he himself left Paris. But the meal went on, one after another the courses would be cleared away, not without having provided Mme de Guermantes with opportunities for clever witticisms or well-judged anecdotes. Meanwhile the poet would go on eating without either the duke or duchess showing any sign of remembering that he was a poet. And presently the luncheon would come to an end and the party would break up, without a word having been said about poetry which they nevertheless all admired but to which, by a reserve analogous to that of which Swann had given me a foretaste, no one referred. This reserve was simply a matter of good form. But for the fellow guest, if he thought about the matter, there was something strangely melancholy about it all, and these meals in the Guermantes household were reminiscent of the

"One day, when she had gone out with a handkerchief tied round her head and a loaf of bread in her hand, Jean met her. "I am just off to feed my peacocks; won't you come with me?" she said in a somewhat absent-minded voice." (Above)

"The being which had been reborn in me when with a sudden shudder of happiness I had heard the noise common to the spoon touching the plate and the hammer striking the wheel, or had felt, beneath my feet, the unevenness common to the paving-stones of the Guermantes courtyard and to those of the baptistery of St Mark's, this being is nourished only by the essences of things, in these alone does it find its sustenance and delight."

LUNCH AT REVEILLON

Scrambled eggs with bacon

Lobster American style

Hare à l'allemande

Rose and macaroon preserve

hours which timid lovers often spend together in talking trivialities until it is time to part, without – whether form shyness, from modesty or from awkwardness – the great secret which they would have been happier to confess ever having succeeded in passing from their hearts to their lips. (The Guermantes Way)

Although, on entering the world of the Guermantes, the narrator has the impression that he is close to the essence of things, he still feels an undefinable lack. Of course, the showy luxury and artistic raptures of Mme Verdurin suddenly appear ridiculous, compared with the cultured reserve of the duchess. But is it not just as artificial to feign indifference for the dishes on the table as to make them the center of conversation? Marcel has a feeling that there must be a middle way between conversation which makes the guests forget what is on their plates and involved discussions of recipes which overrides all else. But as he listens to the duchess, the hero savours her vocabulary, as if it were a meal in itself, it was: *as richly flavoured as those dishes which it is possible to come across in the delicious books of Pampille, but which have in real life become so rare, dishes in which the jellies, the butter, the gravy, the quenelles are all genuine and unalloyed, in which even the salt is brought specially from the salt-marshes of Brittany: from her accent, her choice of words, one felt that*

the basis of the duchess's conversation came directly from Guermantes. (The Guermantes Way)

The authenticity of the ingredients is matched by the authenticity of the words she chooses. A term which would be judged "vulgar" by the snobs is the hallmark of speech that conserves the piquancy and freshness of its origins. The worldly ritual of the dinner party then assumes the solemnity of a Last Supper. From the apex of the social pyramid, which he has at last attained, the budding writer has a premonition of the direction his art will take:

In the period that followed I was continually to be invited, however small the party, to these repasts at which I at one time imagined the guests as seated like the Apostles in the Sainte-Chapelle. They did assemble there indeed, like the early Christians, not to partake merely of a material nourishment, which was incidentally exquisite, but in a sort of social Eucharist; so that in the course of a few dinner parties I assimilated the acquaintance of all the friends of my hosts, friends to whom they presented me with a tinge of benevolent patronage so marked (as a person for whom they had always had a sort of parental affection) that there was not one among them who would not have felt himself to be somehow failing the duke and duchess if he had given a ball without including my name on his list, and at the same time, while I sipped one of those Yquems which lay concealed in the Guermantes cellars, I tasted ortolans dressed according to a variety of recipes judiciously elaborated and modified by the duke himself. (The Guermantes Way)

"A dish of hot lobster, set in readiness for Mlle de Réveillon who never ate eggs, added to the pleasing smell of zinnias and snapdragon a fragrance which was not, as was theirs, an end in itself, but was destined to add the finishing touch to an anticipated, and more material, form of possession."

The aristocratic forthrightness of the duchess, whose sallies are eagerly awaited by her delighted quests, would seem almost to support the new trends in art to which she has been introduced by Swann – a true connoisseur under his dilettante pose.

But her free-thinking is tempered by the earthy common sense of the duke, for whom a spade is a spade and a picture a picture.

Their traditional idea of art cannot accommodate the bold colors and unconventional subject matter of Elstir's painting. Although they may like him as a man, the truly original artist who dares depict a bundle of asparagus remains a mystery to them. Proust was to receive the same treatment from the real-life characters on whom he modelled the Guermantes social circle.

I know of course that they're merely sketches, but still, I don't feel myself that he puts enough work into them. Swann had the nerve to try and make us buy a "Bundle of Asparagus". In fact it was in the house for several days. There was nothing else in the picture, just a bundle of asparagus exactly like the ones you're eating now. But I must say I refused to swallow M. Elstir's asparagus. He wanted three hundred francs for them. Three hundred francs for a bundle of asparagus! A louis, that's as much as they're worth, even early in the season. I thought it a bit stiff. (...)

"I believe you know M. Elstir," the duchess said to me. *"As a man, he's quite pleasant."*

"He's intelligent," said the duke. *"You're surprised, when you talk to him, that his paintings should be so vulgar."* (...)

"Didn't he once start a portrait of you, Oriane?" asked the princess de Parme.

"Yes, in shrimp pink," replied Mme de Guermantes," *but that's not going to make his name live for posterity. It's a ghastly thing; Basin wanted to have it destroyed."* (...)

M. de Guermantes having declared (following upon Elstir's asparagus and those that had just been served after the chicken financière) that green asparagus grown in the open air, which, as has been so quaintly said by the charming writer who signs herself E. de Clermont-Tonnerre, "have not the impressive rigidity of their sisters," ought to be eaten with eggs. "One man's meat is another man's poison, as they say," replied *M. de Bréauté. "In the province of Canton, in China, the*

greatest delicacy that can be set before one is a dish of completely rotten ortolan's eggs." (...)

"I think it must be charming, a country where you can be quite sure that your dairyman will supply you with really rotten eggs, eggs of the year of the comet. I can just see myself dipping my bread and butter in them. I may say that it sometimes happens at aunt Madeleine's" (Mme de Villeparisis's) *"that things are served in a state of putrefaction, eggs included."* Then, as Mme d'Arpajon protested, *"But my dear Phili, you know it as well as I do. You can see the chicken in the egg. (...) It's not an omelette you get there, it's a regular chicken-run, but at least it isn't marked on the menu. You were so wise not to come to dinner there the day before yesterday, there was a brill cooked in carbolic! I assure you, it wasn't a dinner table, it was far more like an isolation ward. Really, Norpois carries loyalty to the pitch of heroism: he had a second helping!"* (The Guermantes Way)

These dinner parties sparkling with wit are punctuated by the learned interventions of Hannibal de Bréauté, accepted as curiosities in a world where good taste dictates that one should appear to be ignorant. "What a goose; what a country bumpkin I am," the duchess likes to proclaim, while over the dessert her cousin informs her that:

The flavour of vanilla we tasted in the excellent ice you gave us this evening, duchess, comes from a plant called the vanilla tree. (...)

"Babal, you're divine, you know everything," cried the duchess. (The Guermantes Way)

Ennobled by the aristocratic setting of the Guermantes dining table, the asparagus from Combray is served up in a multitude of ways, establishing a counterpoint with the dinners of the narrator's childhood and hinting at a truth near at hand, to which the Guermantes set can nevertheless never give him access. The duchess's wit is dissipated in a spate of amusing anecdotes.

Proust the novelist, on the other hand, was to bring out the full flavour of the stories he picked up when dining in town. He knew how to capture the verve of Oriane de Guermantes, as during this dinner given in honour of the princesse de Parme, at which she makes fun of her cousin Zénaïde d'Heudicourt's

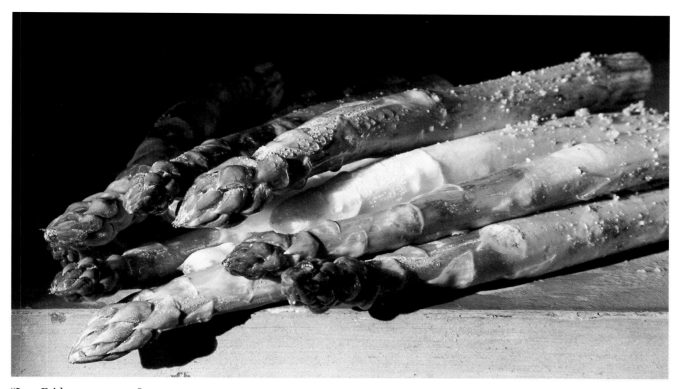

"Last Friday, as soon as I received your note giving me your permission to do so, I sent a clever arrangement of fruit to Madame la Duchesse. (I say clever because I devised it myself, and I believe this is how authors are accustomed to describing their own work.) Did it arrive safely? You would have recognized it by the large bunch of asparagus that I used as a centrepiece. Asparagus is a vegetable which I greatly admire, as you will see in my book if you read it."
(Marcel Proust to Armand de Guiche, 1909)

LUNCH WITH THE DUKE AND DUCHESS DE GUERMANTES

Green asparagus with soft-boiled eggs

Ortolans

Chicken in Madeira and truffle source

Salad

Vanilla ice-cream

stinginess. Little does she know that she herself is frittering away an inheritance, the value of which is perceived only by the narrator. Proust's genius is to give these genuine ingredients a new vigour and observe them with the eye of Elstir painting a bundle of asparagus.

"I should explain to your Royal Highness," went on the duke, "that Oriane's cousin may be superior, good, stout, anything you like to mention, but she is not exactly – what shall I say – lavish."

"Yes, I know, she's terribly close-fisted," broke in the princess.

"I should not have ventured to use the expression, but you have hit on exactly the right word. It's reflected in her house-keeping, and especially in the cooking, which is excellent, but strictly rationed." (…)

"All the same, one must admit that the fare you get there is of the very best," (…) "I don't know any house where one eats better."

"Or less," put in the duchess.

"It's quite wholesome and quite adequate for what you would call a vulgar yokel like myself," went on the duke. "One doesn't outrun one's appetite."

"Oh, if it's to be taken as a cure (…). It's certainly more healthy than sumptuous. (…)

"The cooking at Zénaïde's is not bad, but you would think it more ordinary if she was less parsimonious. There are some things her cook does quite well, and others he doesn't bring off. I've had some thoroughly bad dinners there, as in most houses, only they've done me less harm there because the stomach is, after all, more sensitive to quantity than to quality."

"Well, to get on with the story," the duke concluded, "Zénaïde insisted that Oriane should go to luncheon there, and, as my wife is not very fond of going out anywhere she resisted, wanted to be sure that under the pretence of a quiet meal she was not being trapped into some great junket (…). 'You must come,' Zénaïde insisted, boasting of all the good things there would be to eat. 'You're going to have a purée of chestnuts, I need say no more than that, and there will be seven little bouchées à la reine.' 'Seven little bouchées!' cried Oriane, 'that means that we shall be at least eight!'" (The Guermantes Way)

Marcel Proust at Amphion, home of the princess Brancovan. Front row: the princesse de Caraman-Chimay and Abel Herman; second row: Mme de Montegnard, the princesse de Polignac and the comtesse Mathieu de Noailles; back row: prince Edmond de Polignac, the princess Brancovan, Marcel Proust, Brancovan, Mme X and Léon Delafosse. (Opposite)

"The roses of Réveillon... like painted flowers upon the surface of the porcelain stands in which they were arranged, (...) reflected on the white-panelled walls, they produced the impression of motionless designs, as blue as hycinths, as red as roses."

AT THE SEASIDE

Paul Helleu, Young woman with parasol on a jetty, Musée des Arts Décoratifs, Paris.

"We had now come in sight of the hotel, with its lights (...) now protective and kind, speaking to us of home."

"At night they did not dine in the hotel, where, hidden springs of electricity flooding the great dining-room with light, it became as if it were an immense and wonderful aquarium..." (Opposite)

Drawing on his experience of Houlgate, Dieppe, Trouville and Cabourg, and other sea and lakeside holidays spent in Brittany, Holland, Geneva, even Venice, Marcel Proust composed an idealized seaside resort in Normandy: the Balbec of *Within a Budding Grove*. In the years 1907 to 1914, when he was writing his book, the author was a frequent visitor to the Normandy coast. In fact, the first part of the work was typed at Cabourg's Grand-Hôtel, which he had discovered when it first opened. In August 1907, he wrote to Mme de Caraman-Chimay:

As soon as I heard that the most comfortable hotel on the entire coast was to be found at Cabourg, I went there (...). Since I have been here, I can get up and go out every day, which I have not been able to do for six years.

Balbec, his celebration of the seaside and of youth, is at first – like many dreams come true – something of a disappointment to the young hero:

I found my grandmother in the little train of the local railway which was to take us to Balbec-Plage. (...) She began: "Well, and Balbec?" with a smile so brightly illuminated by her expectation of the great pleasure which she supposed me to have experienced that I dared not at once confess to her my disappointment. (...) But how much more were my sufferings increased when we had finally landed in the hall of the Grand Hotel at Balbec, and I stood there in front of the monumental staircase of imitation marble, while my grandmother, regardless of the growing hostility and contempt of the strangers among whom we were about to live, discussed "terms" with the manager, a pot-bellied figure with a face and a voice alike covered with scars (left by the excision of countless pustules from the one, and from the other of the divers accents acquired from an alien ancestry and a cosmopolitan upbringing), a smart dinner-jacket, and the air of a psychologist who, whenever the "omnibus" discharged a fresh load, invariably took the grandees for haggling skinflints and the flashy crooks for grandees! (...) I was astonished to find (...) that the torture chamber which a new place of residence is could appear to some people a "delightful abode," to quote the hotel prospectus, which might perhaps exaggerate but was none the less addressed to a whole army of clients to whose tastes it must appeal. True, it invoked, to make them come to the Grand Hotel, Balbec, not only the "exquisite fare" and the "magical view across the Casino gardens," but also the "ordinances of
Her Majesty Queen Fashion, which no one may violate with impunity without being taken for a philistine, a charge that no well-bred man would willingly incur." (Within a Budding Grove)

The wind, a familiar force in the life of the child at Combray, here accentuates the sense of social unease felt by the adolescent. By allowing the bracing sea breeze to disturb the conventional atmosphere of the hotel dining-room, the narrator's grandmother upsets the artificial order of life in a provincial holiday resort:

This dining-room at Balbec – bare-walled, filled with a sunlight green as the water in a pond, while a few feet away from it the high tide and broad daylight erected as though before the gates of the heavenly city an indestructible and mobile rampart of emerald and gold – differed from our dining-room at Combray which gave on to the houses across the street. At Combray, since we were known to everyone, I took heed of no one. In seaside life one does not know one's neighbors. (...) Nor had I acquired the more noble indifference which a man of the world would have felt towards the people who were eating in the dining-room or the boys and girls who strolled past the window, with whom I was pained by the thought that I should never be allowed to go on expeditions. (...) I followed all their movements through the transparency of that great bay of glass which allowed so much light to flood the room. But it intercepted the wind, and this was a defect in the eyes of my grandmother, who, unable to endure the thought that I was losing the benefit of an hour in the open air, surreptitiously opened a pane and at once sent flying, together with the menus, the newspapers, veils and hats of all the people at the other tables, while she herself, fortified by the celestial draught, remained calm and smiling like Saint Blandina amid the torrent of invective which, increasing my sense of isolation and misery, those contemptuous, dishevelled, furious visitors combined to pour on us. (Within a Budding Grove)

Quite unaffected by outside judgements of her, his grandmother has the quiet serenity and firm courage of all those who know they are doing what is right. Entirely devoted to the health of her grandchild, she does not share his worries about being accepted into the polite society of the hotel.

This little group in the Balbec hotel looked at each new arrival with suspicion, and, while affecting to take not the

least interest in him, hastened, all of them, to interrogate their friend the head waiter about him. For it was the same head waiter – Aimé – who returned every year for the season, and kept their tables for them; and their lady-wives, having heard that his wife was "expecting," would sit after meals working each at one of the "tiny garments," stoppping only to put up their glasses and stare at my grandmother and myself because we were eating hard-boiled eggs in salad, which was considered common and was "not done" in the best society of Alençon. (Within a Budding Grove)

A liking for fresh air and hard-boiled eggs in one's salad are family traditions which appear suspect to the arbiters of provincial taste, and they look down their noses at the new arrivals. But the sense of social ostracism is made up for by Marcel's discovery of the wonderful seascapes. At Balbec, the lesson in simplicity given by his grandmother is combined with an intoxicating revelation; reality is itself an inexhaustible source of poetry, and it is in contemplating it that one becomes an artist:

When, in the morning, the sun came from behind the hotel, disclosing to the sands bathed in light as far as the first bastions of the sea, it seemed to be showing me another side of the picture, and to be inviting me to pursue, along the winding path of its rays, a motionless but varied journey amid all the fairest scenes of the diversified landscape of the hours. And on this first morning, it pointed out to me far off, with a jovial finger, those blue peaks of the sea which bear no name on any

"I could well appreciate the charm that this great hotel might have for certain persons. It was arranged like a theatre, and was filled to the wings with a numerous and animated cast."

Trouville at the turn of the century, a drawing by Edmond-Emile Gotorbe.

map, until, dizzy with its sublime excursion over the thundering and chaotic surface of their crests and avalanches, it came to take shelter from the wind in my bedroom, lolling across the unmade bed and scattering its riches over the splashed surface of the basin-stand and into my open trunk, where, by its very splendour and misplaced luxury, it added still further to the general impression of disorder. Alas for that sea wind: an hour later, in the big dining-room — while we were having lunch, and from the leathern gourd of a lemon were sprinkling a few golden drops on to a pair of soles which presently left on our plates the plumes of their picked skeletons, curled like stiff feathers and resonant as citherns, — it seemed to my grandmother a cruel deprivation not to be able to feel its life-giving breath on her cheek, on account of the glass partition, transparent but closed, which, like the front of a glass case in a museum, separated us from the beach while allowing us to look out upon its whole expanse, and into which the sky fitted so completely that its azure had the effect of being the color of the windows and its white clouds so many flaws in the glass. Imagining that I was "sitting on the mole" or at rest in the "boudoir" of which Baudelaire speaks, I wondered whether his "sun's rays upon the sea" were not — a very different thing from the evening ray, simple and superficial as a tremulous golden shaft — just what at that moment was scorching the sea topaz-yellow, fermenting it, turning it pale and milky like beer, frothy like milk, while now and then there hovered over it great blue shadows which, for his own amusement, some god seemed to be shifting to and fro by moving a mirror in the sky. (Within a Budding Grove)

A meeting with Madame de Villeparisis, née Madeleine de Bouillon, who is staying at the Grand-Hôtel with her entire household, is the writer's cue to insert, almost word for word, some notes he had once written on the painter Chardin. It was Chardin's painting — opulent and full-bodied — that had revealed to Proust the beauty of a life he found tasteless and thought of as dull.

At table with Madame de Villeparisis — an old friend of his grandmother's and an exponent of the same virtues of simplicity and discretion — Marcel rises above the worldly pomp of the hotel setting to see with the eyes of Chardin, an artist who had managed to depict *that sad and mundane moment when one has just finished lunch but when the table has not yet been completely cleared.*

Now, the young man is initiated into the great art of the commonplace: the meals set before them are transformed into sumptuous still lifes:

Mme de Villeparisis tactfully made as if to leave my grandmother to herself after the first greetings, but my grandmother insisted on staying to talk to her until lunch-time, being anxious to discover how her friend managed to get her letters earlier than we got ours, and to get such nice grilled dishes (for Mme de Villeparisis, who took a keen interest in her food, had the poorest opinion of the hotel kitchen which served us with meals that my grandmother, still quoting Mme de Sévigné, described as "of a sumptuousness to make you die of hunger"). And the marquise formed the habit of coming every day, while waiting to be served, to sit down for a moment at our table in the dining-room, insisting that we should not rise from our chairs or in any way put ourselves out. At the most we would occasionally linger, after finishing our lunch, to chat to her, at that sordid moment when the knives are left littering the tablecloth among crumpled napkins. For my own part, in order to preserve (so that I might be able to enjoy Balbec) the idea that I was on the uttermost promontory of the earth, I compelled myself to look farther afield, to notice only the sea, to seek in it the effects described by Baudelaire and to let my gaze fall upon our table only on days when there was set on it some gigantic fish, some marine monster, which unlike the knives and forks was contemporary with the primitive epochs in which the Ocean first began to teem with life, at the time of the Cimmerians, a fish whose body with its numberless vertebrae, its blue and pink veins, had been constructed by nature, but according to an architectural plan, like a polychrome cathedral of the deep. (Within a Budding Grove)

In *Remembrance of Things Past*, it is Elstir, painter of the "Asparagus" which so disconcerted the Guermantes, who introduces the hero to the beauty of the visible world. Elstir, the archetype of all painters, lives near Balbec. The meeting with him is a turning point and, when the holiday is over, the hero understands that still life becomes living nature and that like life itself, it will always have something new to tell us:

I would now happily remain at the table while it was being cleared, and, if it was not a moment at which the girls of the little band might be passing, it was no longer solely towards the sea that I would turn my eyes. Since I had seen such things depicted in water-colors by Elstir, I sought to find

"Chardin will have been a man who merely took delight in his dining-room, amidst the fruit and the glasses, but as a man of a keener awareness, his delight too intense so that it overflowed into unctuous brushstrokes and immortal pigments."
Jean-Baptiste Chardin, Grapes and Pomegranates, Musée du Louvre, Paris. (Below)
"The marine dining-room of Balbec, with its damask linen prepared like altar-cloths to receive the setting sun." (Overleaf)

"And, in fact, the chocolate soufflés arrived at their destination unspilled..."

again in reality, I cherished as though for their poetic beauty, the broken gestures of the knives still lying across one another, the swollen convexity of a discarded napkin into which the sun introduced a patch of yellow velvet, the half-empty glass which thus showed to greater advantage the noble sweep of its curved sides and, in the heart of its translucent crystal, clear as frozen daylight, some dregs of wine, dark but glittering with reflected lights, the displacement of solid objects, the transmutation of liquids by the effect of light and shade, the shifting colors of the plums which passed from green to blue and from blue to golden yellow in the half-plundered dish, the chairs, like a group of old ladies, that came twice daily to take their places round the white cloth spread on the table as on an altar at which were celebrated the rites of the palate, and where in the hollows of the oyster-shells a few drops of lustral water had remained as in tiny holy water stoups of stone; I tried to find beauty there where I had never imagined before that it could exist, in the most ordinary things, in the profundities of "still life." (Within a Budding Grove)

It now remains for him to work out the "recipe" of his style, which draws just as much on a painter's palette as on the delectable science of a cordon-bleu chef, mixing the visible, intoxicating and disparate ingredients of daily life to make palpable the atmosphere of, for instance, his grandmother's bedroom:

Hers did not look out directly on the sea, as mine did, but was open on three of its four sides — on to a strip of the esplanade, a courtyard, and a view of the country inland — and was furnished differently from mine, with armchairs embroidered with metallic filigree and pink flowers from which the cool and pleasant odour that greeted one on entering seemed to emanate. And at that hour when the sun's rays, drawn from different exposures and, as it were, from different hours of the day, broke the angles of the wall, projected on to the chest of drawers, side by side with a reflection of the beach, a festal altar as variegated as a bank of field-flowers, hung on the fourth wall the folded, quivering, warm wings of a radiance ready at any moment to resume its flight, warmed like a bath a square of provincial carpet before the window overlooking the courtyard which the sun festooned and patterned like a climbing vine, and added to the charm and complexity of the room's furniture by seeming to pluck and scatter petals of the silken flowers on the chairs and to make their silver threads stand out from the fabric, this room in which I lingered for a moment before going to get ready for our drive suggested a prism in which the colors of the light that shone outside were broken up, a hive in which the sweet juices of the day which I was about to taste were distilled, scattered, intoxicating and visible, a garden of hope which dissolved in a quivering haze of silver threads and rose petals. But before all *this I had drawn back my own curtains, impatient to know what Sea it was that was playing that morning by the shore, like a Nereid. For none of those Seas ever stayed with us longer than a day. The next day there would be another, which sometimes resembled its predecessor. But I never saw the same one twice. (Within a Budding Grove)*

In the way their colors change, fruits and the sea itself make us aware of the passage of time, chief protagonist of Proust's work:

We had several times, in the last few days, seen driving past us in a stately equipage, tall, red-haired, handsome, with a rather prominent nose, the princesse de Luxembourg, who was staying in the neighborhood for a few weeks. Her carriage had stopped outside the hotel, a footman had come in and spoken to the manager, had gone back to the carriage and had reappeared with the most amazing armful of fruit (which combined a variety of seasons in a single basket, like the bay itself) with a card: "la princesse de Luxembourg," on which were scrawled a few words in pencil. For what princely traveller, sojourning here incognito, could they be intended, those plums, glaucous, luminous and spherical as was at that moment the circumfluent sea, those transparent grapes clustering on the shrivelled wood, like a fine day in autumn, those pears of a heavenly ultramarine? For it could not be on my grandmother's friend that the princess meant to pay a call.

DINNER WITH ROBERT DE SAINT-LOUP

Oysters

Bass in court-bouillon

Pauillac Lamb

Apples à l'anglaise

Individual chocolate soufflés

"... in the evening (...) I had been led by some effect of sunlight to mistake what was only a darker stretch of sea for a distant coastline, or to gaze delightedly at a belt of liquid azure without knowing whether it belonged to sea or sky."

And yet on the following evening Mme de Villeparisis sent us the bunch of grapes, cool, liquid, golden, and plums and pears which we remembered too, though the plums had changed, like the sea at our dinner-hour, to a dull purple, and in the ultramarine of the pears there floated the shapes of a few pink clouds. (Within a Budding Grove)

But it is across the bay, at the Rivebelle restaurant, that the narrator celebrates his new birth, as a writer. Marcel dines there in the company of Mme de Villparisis's nephew, Robert de Saint-Loup, whose casual elegance and polished simplicity he much admires:

But when we arrived at Rivebelle, immediately — what with the excitement of a new pleasure, and finding myself in that different zone into which the exceptional introduces us after having cut the thread, patiently spun throughout so many days, that was guiding us towards wisdom — as though there were never to be any such thing as tomorrow, nor any lofty aims to be realized, all that precise machinery of prudent hygiene which had been working to safeguard them vanished. A waiter was offering to take my coat, whereupon Saint-Loup asked: "You're sure you won't be cold? Perhaps you'd better keep it: it's not very warm in here."

"No, no," I assured him, and perhaps I did not feel the cold; but however that might be, I no longer knew the fear of falling ill, the necessity of not dying, the importance of work. I gave up my coat; we entered the dining-room to the sound of some warlike march played by the gipsy band, we advanced between two rows of tables laid for dinner as along an easy path of glory, and, feeling a happy glow imparted to our bodies by the rhythms of the band which conferred on us these military honors, this unmerited triumph, we concealed it beneath a grave and frozen mien, beneath a languid, casual gait, so as not to be like those music-hall "mashers" who, wedding a ribald verse to a patriotic air, come running on to the stage with the martial countenance of a victorious general.

From that moment I was a new man, who was no longer my grandmother's grandson and would remember her only when it was time to get up and go, but the brother, for the time being, of the waiters who were going to bring us our dinner. (Within a Budding Grove)

I felt cut off (...) from all external preoccupations (...) by the savour of the exquisite dishes that were set before us. These gave as much pleasure to my imagination as to my palate;

TEA-TIME WITH ALBERTINE

Cheese sandwiches

Apple tart

Apricot tartlets

Cider

"These "Madame Laudet Sundays" when the weather was fine reached their high point round about five o'clock. With the pleasure that she felt at seeing all the tables in the open air packed full, went the satisfaction of the shopkeeper whose business is thriving (...) and something like a modest pride at finding herself surrounded by so many kindly folk, and at being able to wield such power."
Marcel Proust on an outing in the country. (Opposite)

sometimes the little piece of nature from which they had been extracted, the rugged holy-water stoup of the oyster in which lingered a few drops of brackish water, or the gnarled stem, the yellowed branches of a bunch of grapes, still enveloped them, inedible, poetic and distant as a landscape, evoking as we dined successive images of a siesta in the shade of a vine or of an excursion on the sea; on other evenings it was the cook alone who brought out these original properties of the viands, presenting them in their natural setting, like works of art, and a fish cooked in a court-bouillon was brought in on a long earthenware platter, on which, standing out in relief on a bed of bluish herbs, intact but still contorted from having been dropped alive into boiling water, surrounded by a ring of satellite shell-fish, of animalcules, crabs, shrimps and mussels, it had the appearance of a ceramic dish by Bernard Palissy. (The Guermantes Way)

Forgetting the strict diet imposed on him by his delicate state of health, forgetting the social barriers separating him from the waiters, and oblivious to family honor, Marcel feels his surroundings expand to universal dimensions. Drunkenness turns the tables into swirling celestial bodies, and the euphoria of having transgressed the social norms transforms him into a superman in the midst of a narrow-minded crowd:

The dose of beer, and a fortori of champagne, which at Balbec I should not have ventured to take in a week, albeit to my calm and lucid consciousness the savour of those beverages represented a pleasure clearly appreciable if easily sacrificed, I now imbibed at a sitting, adding to it a few drops of port which I was too bemused to be able to taste, and I gave the violinist who had just been playing the two louis which I had been saving up for the last month with a view to buying something, I could not remember what. Several of the waiters, let loose among the tables, were flying along at full speed, each carrying on his outstretched palm a dish which it seemed to be the object of this kind of race not to let fall. And in fact the chocolate soufflés arrived at their destination unspilled, the potatoes à l'anglaise, in spite of the gallop that must have given them a shaking, arranged as at the start round the Pauillac lamb. (...) Presently the spectacle settled down, in my eyes at least, into an order at once more noble and more calm. All this dizzy activity became fixed in a quiet harmony. I looked at the round tables whose innumerable assemblages

filled the restaurant like so many planets, as the latter are represented in old allegorical pictures. Moreover, there seemed to be some irresistible force of attraction at work among these divers stars, and at each table the diners had eyes only for the tables at which they were not sitting, with the possible exception of some wealthy amphitryon who, having managed to secure a famous author, was endeavouring to extract from him, thanks to the magic properties of the turning-table, a few insignificant remarks at which the ladies marvelled. The harmony of these astral tables did not prevent the incessant revolution of the countless waiters who, because instead of being seated like the diners were on their feet, performed their gyrations in a more exalted sphere. No doubt they were running, one to fetch the hors d'oeuvre, another to change the wine or to bring clean glasses. But despite these special reasons, their perpetual course among the round tables yielded, after a time, to the observer the law of its dizzy but ordered circulation. Seated behind a bank of flowers, two horrible cashiers, busy with endless calculations, seemed two witches occupied in forecasting by astrological signs the disasters that might from time to time occur in this celestial vault fashioned according to the scientific conceptions of the Middle Ages.

And I rather pitied all the diners because I felt that for

them the round tables were not planets and that they had not cut through the scheme of things in such a way as to be delivered from the bondage of habitual appearances and enabled to perceive analogies. They thought that they were dining with this or that person, that the dinner would cost roughly so much, and that tomorrow they would begin all over again. (Within a Budding Grove)

Friendship with Saint-Loup is followed by acquaintance with a group of girls, reawakening memories of tea-parties with Gilberte Swann. It is Elstir who introduces him to the young lady he finds the most attractive: Albertine.

That day, (...) I was sorry that Saint-Loup was not at Balbec. I had seen some young women, who at a distance had seemed to me lovely, (...) I seemed to see charming women all round me, because I was too tired, if it was on the beach, too shy if it was in the Casino or at a pastry-cook's, to go anywhere near them. And yet, (...) I should have liked to know beforehand what the prettiest girls that life had to offer looked like at close quarters, (...) I should have had the courage to enter the ballroom if Saint-Loup had been with me. Left by myself, I was simply hanging about in front of the Grand Hotel until it was time for me to join my grandmother, when,

"The day after tomorrow we're going to Harambouville in the carriage. It's a magnificent drive, the cider is delicious, (...) I'll give you some Norman pancakes." (Opposite).

"How often in Paris, during the month of May (...) was I to buy a branch of apple-blossom from the florist and afterwards spend the night with its flowers in which bloomed the same creamy essence that still powdered with its froth the burgeoning leaves..." (Right).

still almost at the far end of the esplanade, along which they projected a striking patch of color, I saw five or six young girls as different in appearance and manner from all the people one was accustomed to see at Balbec (...).

When Elstir asked me to come with him so that he might introduce me to Albertine, who was sitting a little further down the room, I first of all finished eating a coffee éclair and, with a show of keen interest, asked an old gentleman whose acquaintance I had just made (and to whom I thought that I might offer the rose in my buttonhole which he had admired) to tell me more about the old Norman fairs. (...)

I returned home thinking of that party, of the coffee éclair which I had finished eating before I let Elstir take me up to Albertine, the rose which I had given the old gentleman, all the details selected unbeknownst to us by the circumstances of the occasion, which compose for us, in a special and quite fortuitous order, the picture we retain of a first meeting. (Within a Budding Grove)

On picnics with his new friends, the narrator refuses to be moved by their amazement at his odd tastes, just as his grandmother has remained faithful to her love of fresh air and hard-boiled eggs. There, enjoying his new-felt passion, the wind on the cliff-tops and the cakes of fond memory, he consumates his entry into the realms of both love and art:

I ordered the cheese or salad sandwiches or sent out for the cakes which I would eat on the cliff with the girls (...). Then, (...) the sandwiches ready, I went to join Albertine, Andrée, Rosemonde, and any others there might be, and we would set out on foot or on our bicycles. (...) There were days when we picnicked at one of the outlying farms which catered for visitors. (...) But at other times, instead of going to a farm, we would climb to the highest point of the cliff, and, when we had reached it and were seated on the grass, would undo our parcel of sandwiches and cakes. My friends preferred the sandwiches, and were surprised to see me eat only a single chocolate cake, sugared with gothic tracery, or an apricot tart. This was because, with the sandwiches of cheese or salad, a form of food that was novel to me and was ignorant of the past, I had nothing in common. But the cakes understood, the tarts were talkative. There was in the former an insipid taste of cream, in the latter a fresh taste of fruit which knew all ... (Within a Budding Grove)

"It was definitely a Sunday tart, gazed at with admiration and eaten with relish on those Sunday noons, with the narrow street outside on the same level as the room and the sky purplish-blue when the weather was stormy, or aflicker with gold when the sun was shining." (Opposite)

"The chief reason for going to the farm when they felt the need of a little refreshment was a wish to see her and to be in her home, much as some people frequent certain restaurants, though the reason they give may be that the cider is better there than elsewhere or the cheese particularly good." (Overleaf)

DINING WITH PROUST

Marcel Proust in 1896, in the days when he would give select literary dinner parties at his parents' apartment, 45 rue de Courcelles.

"How pleasant a museum is dinner, (...) when the color of the wine gleams like the glow of a picture (...) dishes of silver set upon a dazzling cloth, so that in the space of a single hour we receive the full, direct sensation of many masterpieces, of which the desire of one alone suffiices to fill with charm the lazy hour when appetite is slowly growing."

For many years, the son of the celebrated Dr Proust stayed out late. In the society salons of turn-of-the-century Paris, in the fashionable brasseries and restaurants, he was a familiar figure: delicate, starry-eyed, eager to please – an oriental prince with a caressing tone of voice. Sending out orders and counter-orders in a bewildering stream of letters, notes and "petits bleus", he would invite his guests to meet him at Ciros's, Weber's and especially Larue's, on the corner of the place de la Madeleine and the rue Royale. These were the high places of a brilliant, wealthy young man of good taste. He would dine there with his cronies, or enjoy a late meal, after the theatre, café-concert or opera, with beautiful actress friends.

Le Gaulois, on 25 May 1897, and *Le Figaro*, the following day, reported:

Yesterday, a literary dinner party of the most elegant kind was given at the home of M. Marcel Proust, who was inviting his many friends for the first time. The guests included: M. Anatole France, comte Louis de Turenne, comte Robert de Montesquiou-Fezensac, de La Gandara, Jean Béraud, G. de Borda, Reynaldo Hahn, etc.

The marquis de Castellane, who had been unable to send his apologies, made a brief appearance, but left immediately after dinner to call on his cousin, the prince de Sagan.

M. Marcel Proust's father, the celebrated doctor, had absented himself, leaving his son to perform the honors of a dinner which sparkled with true Parisian wit.

Whether meeting his few intimates or inviting society acquaintances to dine at his parents' house, Marcel Proust always sent out the invitations, worked out the table plan and drew up the menu himself. In doing so, he deployed energy and diplomatic skills worthy of the Quai d'Orsay – and his studies at the Ecole des Sciences Politiques could well have led to a career in diplomacy. But distancing himself from Paris would have been intolerable; and writing demanded his undivided attention. If he could have been attached to a museum or pursued a career in the Fine Arts Department, he would have been well satisfied. Indecisive as he was, he nevertheless passed a competitive examination set by the Ministry of Education and Fine Arts, and was appointed to an unpaid position – which he never took up – as attaché to the Bibliothèque Mazarine. After his parents' death, Proust – a young man who never grew up – entertained only a few close friends at his home, preferring to hold his dinner parties at the Ritz hotel.

Professor Adrien Proust died in 1903. As an act of filial piety, in 1904 Marcel published his first "serious" work (or so he hoped it would be received): a translation of the English art critic John Ruskin's "Amiens Bible". After his mother's death, in 1905, he was grief-stricken for a period of six months, but still managed to publish his second translation of Ruskin, "Sesame and Lilies". He then turned his mind to a number of projects; in 1908, he wrote that he was working on:

A study on the aristocracy
An essay on Saint-Beuve and Flaubert
An essay on Women
An essay on Homosexuality (not easy to publish)
A study on stained glass windows
A study on tombstones
A study on the novel

These early writings all contained elements of his major work, which was provisionally entitled *Time Lost* and *Time Regained*, before finally appearing as *Remembrance of Things Past*.

"The heralding rattle of cold plates being changed for hot ones." (Overleaf)

During the same period, in a notebook he used for jotting down ideas for his novel, Marcel Proust wrote: *How pleasant it is to be alone and cook for oneself.* And, a little further on: *Compare my book with Françoise's beef: it must have absorbed the juice to the very last drop.* Writing the book was comparable to preparing a meal, as he strove to incorporate his experience of life in a highly-wrought stylistic framework. The model he had in mind was the old cook's most perfect creation: Françoise's *boeuf mode*.

The figure of Françoise presides over the development of Proust's novel, just as, at Combray, she presided over her kitchen and its awesome mysteries. And, in exile in Paris, it is she who tells the tale of a lost golden age:

"So it was at Combray itself that you used to be, with a cousin of Madame?" asked the young footman.

"Yes, with Mme Octave – ah, a real saintly woman, I can tell you, and a house where there was always more than enough, and all of the very best – a good woman, and no

"The cold spiced beef with carrots made its appearance, couched by the Michelangelo of our kitchen upon enormous crystals of aspic, like transparent blocks of quartz."

mistake, who didn't spare the partridges, or the pheasants, or anything. You might turn up five to dinner or six, it was never the meat that was lacking, and of the first quality too, and white wine, and red wine, and everything you could wish." (Françoise used the word "spare" in the same sense as La Bruyère.) *"It was she that always paid the damages, even if the family stayed for months and years."* (This reflexion was not really meant as a slur upon us, for Françoise belonged to an epoch when the word "damages" was not restricted to a legal use and meant simply expense.) *"Ah, I can tell you people didn't go away empty from that house."* (*The Guermantes Way*)

In his preface to Brillat-Savarin's *La Physiologie du goût,* Charles Monselet observes that gastronomy is above all a question of spending time. To recapture the flavours of a past age, one must devote long hours to the task. One must withdraw from the flux of time. Thus, on 27 December 1906, in the rooms where his great-uncle, Louis Weil, had died ten years before, Proust began to live the life of a recluse, with no foreseeable end to his labors. Delicate of health, in his apartments on the boulevard Haussman and latterly his room in the rue Hamelin, he led a feverish nocturnal existence, isolated from noise and from cooking smells, which triggered off terrible attacks of asthma.

Céleste Albaret, who served Proust from 1914 to 1922, says of this period:

At the very beginning, before the war, he did eat a little from time to time. He would ask Nicolas to cook him a sole or to order a dish or a delicacy from a restaurant. In fact, with very rare exceptions, all Nicholas and Céline's own food came in from outside so that there could be no smell of cooking. There was a good plain restaurant, the Louis XVI, nearby on boulevard Haussman; the Cottins' food came from there. M. Proust's came from Larue's, which no longer exists but was once a famous and fashionable restaurant at the corner of rue Royale and place de la Madeleine, where M. Proust had often dined and had supped with friends. Finally, at the beginning of the war, he used to go to the restaurant of the Ritz.

Anything he wanted Nicolas to bring him he usually asked for if he had had his coffee at about two or three o'clock in the afternoon. Nicolas would serve the sole or the dish from the restaurant at five or six o'clock. (...) But it was mostly whim (...). Anyway, M. Proust's demands were not

complicated. *He was simple in his taste for food as in everything – but it had to be prepared exactly to his liking. He was a connoisseur, or rather, he had been one. I could see that his fancies were really sudden memories.*
(Céleste Albaret, *Monsieur Proust*)

The faithful Céleste was also to win a place in her master's great work. She appears, under her own name, as one of the servants at Balbec:

Difficult as it was for a guest to penetrate to the servants' quarters, and vice versa, I had very soon formed a mutual bond of friendship, as strong as it was pure, with these two young persons, Mlle Marie Gineste and Mme Céleste Albarat. (...) They often came in the morning to see me when I was still in bed. (...) while I dipped croissants in my milk, Céleste would say to me: "Oh! little black devil with raven hair, oh deep-dyed mischief! I don't know what your mother was thinking of when she made you, you're just like a bird. Look, Marie, wouldn't you say he was preening his feathers, and the supple way he turns his head right round, he looks so light, you'd think he was just learning to fly. Ah! it's lucky for you that you were born into the ranks of the rich, otherwise what would ever have become of you, spendthrift that you are. Look at him throwing away his croissant because it touched the bed. There he goes, now, look, he's spilling his milk. Wait till I tie a napkin round you, because you'll never do it for yourself, I've never seen anyone so helpless and clumsy as you." (Cities of the Plain)

One of Céleste Albaret's daily tasks was in fact to bring Proust his morning coffee and croissant:

I can see it all before me now: the silver coffee pot with his initials; the lidded porcelain jug to keep the boiled milk hot; the big gold-rimmed bowl with the family monogram; the croissant, in its own saucer, from a baker in rue de la Pépinière, opposite rue d'Anjou.

He poured out the coffee himself, but he waited until he was alone. He would make a gesture with his hand, and I would go. But it was easy to work out the proportions of coffee and milk. The coffee pot held the equivalent of two cups, and he poured the equivalent of one and a half cups into his first cup, adding milk to bring it up to about half a litre in all. The milk had to be boiling hot. (...) In fact, the café au lait was meant as a meal. His real nourishment was milk – he sometimes used as much as a litre a day. (...) Apart from his coffee he didn't drink anything – especially not wine. (...)

There is one ridiculous story (...) which says that at a supper at the Ritz, M. Proust drank champagne (...). Nonsense (...). He didn't invite people often and never more than one at a time. (...) For the dinners he gave I had to buy good wines, red or white. (...) Apart from the dinners it was champagne – only Veuve Clicquot – or port...
(Céleste Albaret, *Monsieur Proust*)

The further he progressed with his work, the less Proust ate. The dishes he tended to order were those which evoked memories of the past:

The taste of our breakfast coffee brings with it that vague hope of fine weather which so often long ago, as with the day still intact and full before us, we were drinking out of a bowl of white porcelain (...) suddenly smiled upon us in the pale uncertainty of the dawn. An hour is not merely an hour, it is a vase full of scents and sounds and projects and climates. (Time Regained)

As if echoing his writing, Céleste confirms the fact:

I've already described his memory of Félicie's boeuf à la mode.

"Oh Céleste!" he'd say. "Cold! It was cold I like it best, with the jelly and little carrots..."

Then there was a dish called la petite marmite. The first time he mentioned it I didn't know what it was. And although he knew what it tasted like, he was just as ignorant as I was about the recipe.

"I don't really know how to describe it," he said. "I think you have to mix special bits of beef with chicken gizzards and many other little things. And it has to simmer for a very long time on a low flame. But it's delicious."

I ordered it sometimes from Larue's. I would bring it in, and he ate it out of the pot, never off a plate. He picked at it rather than ate, really – two or three mouthfuls and that was that. When he saw the lid taken off, he didn't even say "There is too much – take some away," or "Keep some for yourself if you like." No, he just had two or three nibbles and then the pot had to be taken away immediately. At the beginning I dared to press him.

"Just a little bit more, Monsieur. What am I going to do with all the rest?"

"Just throw it away, Céleste."

Anyway, he wasn't really keen on any kind of meat. At the most – and that rarely – a bit of chicken.

The dining room at the Ritz hotel.

In latter years, Proust had a private arrangement with this hotel in the place Vendôme, founded by César Ritz. The maître d'hôtel, Olivier Dabescat, would serve him in a separate room and sometimes arranged dinner parties to which Proust invited his friends. The taxi driver Odilon Albaret was allowed to go to the hotel kitchens, even at dead of night, to fetch iced beer for his employer.

But sole, yes, sometimes he would again fancy a sole.

"My dear Céleste, I think I could eat a fried sole. How long do you think it would take, if it is not too much bother?"

"But you can have it right away, Monsieur."

"You are so kind, Céleste!"

There was an excellent fish store nearby, at Félix Potin's on place Saint-Augustin. I'd hurry there, rush back with the sole, fry it, and take it in to him as fast as I could on a large china plate, the fillet resting on a folded clean damask napkin to absorb the fat, with half a lemon at each corner. Just as I'd seen Nicolas do it. Otherwise I would not have known.

Sole was about the only thing he ever finished. Usually, by the time a dish was put in front of him, he no longer wanted it — he had thought about something else in the meantime. Either he picked at it absentmindedly, or he rang and I took it away untouched.

Apart from la petite marmite, chicken, and sole, the only solid foods I saw him touch in eight years was, once, mullet, twice whitebait or eggs, and a few times, Russian salad or fried potatoes. But I never saw him eat even a mouthful of bread, for example.

The mullet had to be small and from Marseilles, and I had to buy them at Prunier's near la Madeleine, because, according to him, nowhere else in Paris was it so fresh and succulent and of the right size. He remembered them because his father had taken the family there sometimes; Prunier's was

also a very good restaurant.
(Céleste Albaret, *Monsieur Proust*)

Jellied beef, the pinnacle of Françoise's culinary achievement, was the piece de résistance of Félicie Fitau, who served the Proust family as cook, when they lived in boulevard Malesherbes, and later rue de Courcelles. When Proust moved to boulevard Haussmann, Céline Cotin, the wife of his valet Nicolas, successfully adopted the recipe, earning her master's praise, as in this letter of 12 July 1909:

Céline,

I send you my warmest congratulations on the wonderful boeuf mode. I only hope that what I am going to do tonight will be as successful, that my style will be as brilliant, clear and substantial as your aspic jelly – that my ideas will have the savour of your carrots and be as nourishing and fresh as your beef. While still working to complete my work of art, I compliment you on yours.

At Combray, when, as a budding writer, he read passages from his favourite authors, Proust's narrator experienced a curious sensation: *I would give myself up to the pleasure of reading their sentences, like a cook who, free of work at last, finds time to enjoy the pleasures of the table.* So Marcel Proust consciously assumed the role of cook as he worked on his novel, and, as he had foretold in his preparatory notes, the work came to have much in common with Françoise's *boeuf mode*: *in a book individual characters, whether human or of some other kind, are made up of numerous impressions derived from many girls, many churches, many sonatas and combined to form a single sonata, a single church, a single girl, so that I should be making my book in the same way that Françoise made that boeuf à la mode which M. de Norpois had found so delicious, just because she had enriched its jelly with so many carefully chosen pieces of meat. (Time Regained)*

Françoise's beef is conceived, prepared and presented as a true masterpiece. In the eyes of the young man, later to become a writer, the cook is a creative genius, and he stands before her as an apprentice: *since the day before, Françoise, rejoicing in the opportunity to devote herself to that art of cooking at which she was so gifted, stimulated, moreover, by the prospect of a new guest, and knowing that she would have to compose, by methods known to her alone, a dish of boeuf à la gelée, had been living in the effervescence of creation. (...) if Françoise was consumed by the burning certainty of creative genius, my lot was the cruel anxiety of the seeker after the truth (...).*

Françoise at the market, searching out the very best ingredients for her masterpiece, is compared with Michelangelo at Carrara: *Since she attached the utmost importance to the intrinsic quality of the materials which were to enter into the fabric of her work, she had gone herself to the Halles to procure the best cuts of rump-steak, shin of beef, calves' feet, just as Michelangelo spent eight months in the mountains of Carrara choosing the most perfect blocks of marble for the monument of Julius II. Françoise expended on these comings and goings so much ardour that Mamma, at the sight of her flaming cheeks, was alarmed lest our old servant should fall ill from overwork, like the sculptor of the Tombs of the Medici in the quarries of Pietrasanta. (Within a Budding Grove)*

"What do I see? A Nesselrode pudding! As well! I declare I shall need a course at Carlsbad after such a Lucullan-feast as this."

Finally... *The cold spiced beef with carrots made its appearance, couched by the Michelangelo of our kitchen upon enormous crystals of aspic, like transparent blocks of quartz.*

With all the flavour of the carrots absorbed into the meat, this dish, masterpiece of a top-flight cook – who is judged worthy to bear comparison with an artist of universal renown – wins unanimous praise:

Françoise received the compliments of M. de Norpois with the proud simplicity, the joyful and (if only momentarily) intelligent expression of an artist when someone speaks to him of his art. (Within a Budding Grove)

Nevertheless, the artist jealously guards the secrets of her creation:

"Well then," inquired my mother," and how do you explain that nobody else can make an aspic as well as you – when you choose?" "I really couldn't say how that becomes about," replied Françoise, who had established no very clear line of demarcation between the verb "to come," in certain of its meanings, and the verb "to become." She was speaking the truth, moreover, if only in part, being scarcely more capable – or desirous – of revealing the mystery which ensured the superiority of her aspics or her creams than a well-dressed woman the secrets of her toilettes or a great singer those of her voice. Their explanations tell us little. (Within a Budding Grove)

Françoise's only revelation has to be read between the lines, when she explains the difference between her *boeuf mode* and that served up in expensive restaurants:

"They do it in too much of a hurry," (...) "and then it's not all done together. You want the beef to become like a sponge, then it will drink up all the juice to the last drop."

In this way, Marcel Proust demonstrates that – for *boeuf mode* no less than for his novel – the secret of creation, the essential ingredient in the maturing of a work of art, is time.

Using another comparison with food, the writer sees himself as a baker, up to his elbows in flour and dough. In one of his preliminary sketches for *Remembrance of Things Past*, he says of his novel: *I shall lay it out on the table, as if I were rolling out pastry.*

Replying to a journalist from *L'Intransigeant*, who had asked him what trade he would take up, if obliged to do so, Proust wrote (in a letter published on 3 August 1920):

DINNER AT THE HOME OF MONSIEUR AND MADAME PROUST

Jellied beef

Baked York ham

Pineapple and truffle salad

Nesselrode pudding

Sir,

You make a distinction between the manual and the spiritual professions to which I am unable to subscribe. For the hand is guided by the spirit.

Our beloved Chardin expressed himself better than I when he said: "We do not paint merely with our hands but with our hearts". And da Vinci, also speaking of painting, referred to it as a "cosa mentale". The same can even be said of love, among other physical activities. That is what makes it so tiring sometimes. I trust you will permit me to use this collaboration of hand and spirit to explain that if I found myself in the situation you describe, I would choose as my manual profession, precisely the profession that I exercise at present, namely that of a writer. And if paper became absolutely unobtainable, then I think I would become a baker, for it is an honorable profession to provide men with their daily bread. Meanwhile, I do my best to create the "bread of angels" of which Racine said (I quote from memory and probably with many inaccuracies):

God Himself compounds it
From his finest wheaten flour
A bread so delectable
Which is not served at the table
Of the company you keep.
I offer it to those who will give
Themselves to me. Do you want to live?
Come. Take and eat!

Marcel Proust kneaded the dough of his "Pain des Anges" (angel bread) through the long night of artistic creativity. We find underlined the note: *Remember: books are the work of solitude and the children of silence.* Working with dreams, words and time, this subtle alchemist distilled into his novel, like drops of light, the transparent substance of our finest hours. He knew that the stuff of books, the substance of our sentences must be spiritual... Transparent like the jelly of Françoise's *boeuf mode*, the substance of Proust's novel sparkles with a soft light, reflecting back to each reader the images he desires to discover in the depths of his own consciousness.

Projecting confidently into the future, this essentially gourmet work contains, like Manet's scandalous and revolutionary picnic, a message of modesty learned from the family cook, a modesty which characterizes all true works of art: *To me it seems more correct to say that the cruel law of art is that people die and we ourselves die after exhausting every form of suffering, so that over our heads may grow the grass not of oblivion but of eternal life, the vigorous and luxuriant growth of a true work of art, and so that thither, gaily and without a thought for those who are sleeping beneath them, future generations may come to enjoy their "déjeuner sur l'herbe". (Time Regained)*

Professor Adrien Proust (1834-1903). This photograph was taken by Paul Nadar on 20 November 1886.

Mme Adrien Proust, née Jeanne Weil (1849-1905). This photograph was taken by Paul Nadar on 5 December 1904.

THE RECIPES

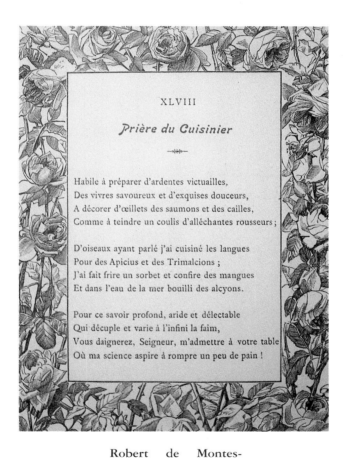

XLVIII

Prière du Cuisinier

Habile à préparer d'ardentes victuailles,
Des vivres savoureux et d'exquises douceurs,
A décorer d'œillets des saumons et des cailles,
Comme à teindre un coulis d'alléchantes rousseurs ;

D'oiseaux ayant parlé j'ai cuisiné les langues
Pour des Apicius et des Trimalcions ;
J'ai fait frire un sorbet et confire des mangues
Et dans l'eau de la mer bouilli des alcyons.

Pour ce savoir profond, aride et délectable
Qui décuple et varie à l'infini la faim,
Vous daignerez, Seigneur, m'admettre à votre table
Où ma science aspire à rompre un peu de pain !

Robert de Montesquiou, Prayer for all, illustrated by Madeleine Lemaire, Paris, Maison Du Livre, 1902.

Aesthete and socialite, Count Robert de Montesquiou (1855-1921) fascinated the young Marcel Proust, although the relationship which developed between them was not without its ups and downs.

STARTERS

"Well, to get on with the story," the Duke concluded, *"Zénaïde insisted that Oriane should go to luncheon there, and as my wife is not very fond of going out anywhere she resisted, and tried in vain to find out who else would be of the party. "You must come," Zénaïde insisted, boasting of all the good things there would be to eat. "You're going to have a purée of chestnuts, I need say no more than that, and there will be seven little bouchées à la reine." "Seven little bouchées!" cried Oriane, "that means that we shall be at least eight!"* (Guermantes Way)

Vol-au-vents

Ingredients: 2 lamb's brains, 5 oz/150 g/5 oz lamb's sweetbreads, 7 oz/200 g/7 oz ready-made puff pastry, 2 oz/50 g/4 tbsp butter, 1 egg yolk, 1¼ oz/30 g 2 tbsp flour, 17 fl oz/500 ml/a good 2 cups chicken stock, 4 fl oz/120 ml/½ cup single cream, 11 oz/300 g/1½ cups button mushrooms, juice of ½ lemon, 4½ oz/125 g/4½ oz cooked chicken, salt and pepper.

Soak the brains and the sweetbreads in cold water for at least 2 hours, changing the water several times. Preheat the oven to 350°F/180°C/gas mark 4. Roll the puff pastry out, then cut into circles 3½ inches/9 cm in diameter, using a pastry cutter or the rim of an upturned glass.

Butter a baking tray lightly, then arrange the pastry circles on it ½ inch (1 cm) apart. Brush with some of the beaten egg yolk, but do not brush the edges as this will prevent the pastry from rising. Using a smaller pastry cutter (about 1 inch/2.5 cm in diameter), mark the 'lid' for each vol-au-vent in the centre of each circle. This should be done very gently taking care not to cut through the pastry. Place in the preheated oven for 15 minutes. Remove from the oven and cut out the lids with the point of a knife. Discard any loose or greasy pastry from the middle of each vol-au-vent using a small spoon.

Melt 1 oz/25 g/2 tbsp of the remaining butter in a heavy-based saucepan and blend in the flour. Cook for 5 minutes, then add the chicken stock. Stir and cook for a further 10 minutes. Stir in the cream and cook for another 10 minutes, then season. Wipe the mushrooms and dry them with a clean cloth, cutting larger ones into small pieces. Melt the remaining butter in a frying pan (skillet). When hot, add the mushrooms, sprinkle with the lemon juice, and simmer until cooked through. Drain the mushrooms and stir the juice into the cream sauce.

Blanch the sweetbreads by placing them in cold water and bringing to the boil. Boil for 5 minutes, then refresh under cold running water. Discard the skin or thin membrane and fat, and cut the flesh into small dice. With your fingers, remove the thin membrane surrounding the brains. Place the brains in a pan, cover with cold salted water, then bring to the boil. Simmer for 5 minutes, then drain and chop into small pieces. Remove any skin from the chicken, and finely dice the meat.

Carefully mix the mushrooms, sweetbreads, brains and chicken into the cream sauce. Simmer for 5 minutes, then adjust the seasoning if necessary. If the filling is too runny, remove from the heat and stir in the remainder of the egg yolk. Do not put back over heat.

Warm up the pastry cases, then arrange them on plates, fill, place lids on top, and serve immediately.

"...between the golden waves of scrambled eggs, of little fleets of bacon, half drowned and barely visible..."

Chairs were pulled up to the table, napkins spread on waiting knees, napkins as fresh and innocent as the joy sparkling in every eye and now enhanced by the discovery, between the golden waves of scrambled eggs, of little fleets of bacon, half drowned and barely visible, which those, now seated, began with a will to rescue from the wreck. (Jean Santeuil)

Scrambled eggs with bacon

Ingredients: 7 oz/200 g/7 oz mild smoked bacon, 12 fresh eggs, 1 tsp/5 ml/1 tsp peanut oil, 1 oz/25 g/2 tbsp butter, 2 tbsp/30 ml/3 tbsp single cream (optional), 1 tsp/5 ml/1 tsp chopped broad-leaved parsley.

Cut the bacon into small strips. Blanch it by placing in a pan of cold water and bringing to the boil. When water is boiling, discard the hot water and replace with cold water. Remove the bacon from the pan using a slotted spoon, dry with a clean cloth and set aside. Break the eggs into a bowl and beat with a fork.

Heat the oil in a frying pan (skillet). When smoking, quickly fry the bacon until crisp, stirring constantly with a wooden spoon. Remove from the pan and drain.

Melt half the butter in a saucepan over a low heat. Add the eggs and bacon and cook gently, stirring constantly. As soon as the eggs become creamy, remove from the heat but keep stirring as they continue to cook. Texture is a matter of taste, but if you feel the eggs are over-cooked add the single cream, and stir in well.

Cut the remaining butter into small pieces and add to the eggs. Pour the scrambled eggs into four ramekins, garnish with chopped parsley and serve immediately.

Serving suggestion: Arrange small croûtons around each ramekin.

But it was lovely all the same just when one was beginning to feel cold and hungry, to return through the village and to see between the trees of the Park light streaming from the windows of the drawing-room and dining-room, and to imagine in anticipation what was already there awaiting one's arrival, though one would not actually see it for several more minutes – the glow of the fire, the table under the lamp, the hot soup in one's plate. (Jean Santeuil)

Cabbage soup with diced bacon

Ingredients: 1 green cabbage, vinegar, 2 garlic cloves, 5 oz/150 g/5 oz smoked bacon, 1 oz/25 g/2 tbsp butter, ½ stock cube, salt and pepper.

Remove the stalk and leaves at the base of the cabbage. Cut cabbage in half, remove the main stem, then chop into 1 inch/2.5 cm pieces. Rinse in a generous quantity of water with a little vinegar (1 tbsp/15 ml/1½ tbsp vinegar to 1¾ pints/1 litre/1 quart water). Drain in a colander. Peel and chop the garlic. Rind and dice the bacon.

Melt the butter in a casserole over a low heat. As soon as it is hot, gently fry the garlic until soft, stirring with a wooden spoon. Do not allow to brown. Add the diced bacon and fry gently for 2 minutes, stirring constantly. Add the cabbage and the crumbled stock cube, then pour in 2½ pints/1.5 litres/6¼ cups water. Season with a little cooking salt and pepper. Cover and cook over a low heat for 45 minutes. The soup should simmer very gently. (If necessary put a heat diffuser under the casserole.) Serve in a warm soup tureen.

Serving suggestion: Serve with fried croûtons.

... I do not know many places in which a simple potato salad is made as it is here with potatoes firm as Japanese ivory buttons and patina'd like those little ivory spoons with which Chinese women sprinkle water over their new-caught fish. (Time Regained)

Potato salad

Ingredients: 1¾ lb/800 g/1¾ lb new or waxy potatoes, salt. *Cream sauce:* 2 tbsp/30 ml/3 tbsp double cream, 1 tsp/5 ml/1 tsp mustard, 1 tsp/5 ml/1 tsp old red wine vinegar, salt and pepper. *Vinaigrette:* 4 tbsp/60 ml/6 tbsp peanut oil, 1 tbsp/15 ml/1½ tbsp white wine vinegar, 1 tbsp/15 ml/1½ tbsp chopped mixed herbs, parsley, chervil and tarragon, salt and pepper. *Cocktail dressing:* 2 egg yolks, 2 fl oz/50 ml/¼ cup peanut oil, 1 tsp/5 ml/1 tsp mustard, 1 tsp/5 ml/1 tsp wine vinegar, 1 tbsp/15 ml/1½ tbsp tomato ketchup, 1 tsp/5 ml/1 tsp brandy, salt and pepper.

Boil the potatoes in their skins in salted water for about 20 minutes. Drain and skin while still hot. Cut into ¼ inch/5 mm slices.

Make up the dressing of your choice and pour over the potatoes. Do not toss using salad servers, as this may damage the potatoes. Hold the salad bowl in both hands and shake. Serve warm.

We could fall upon the omelette and the steak and chips an hour earlier than we were usually allowed to. (Swann's Way)

Mushroom, asparagus and chive omelette

Ingredients: 12 green asparagus spears, 7 oz/200 g/7 oz button mushrooms, 4 oz/100 g/½ cup butter, 10 eggs, salt and pepper, 3 tbsp/45 ml/4½ tbsp chopped chives.

Cut off the woody bases, and peel the asparagus spears. Rinse and cook in boiling water for 8–10 minutes according to size. Plunge into cold water in order to stop cooking and preserve the pleasant green color. Cut off the mushroom stalks level with the caps. Discard stalks or use in the stock pot. Wash caps, slice thinly, and dry with a clean cloth so that they produce a minimum of fluid during cooking. Melt 1½ oz/40 g/3 tbsp of the butter in a frying pan (skillet). When hot, add the mushrooms and sauté over a high heat until slightly browned. Remove from the pan.

Wipe the pan clean with kitchen paper, and melt another 1½ oz/40 g/3 tbsp of the butter. Sauté the asparagus in this until well browned. Finely slice the asparagus spears into rounds, setting the tips aside.

Break the eggs into a bowl, season and beat with a fork. Add the mushrooms and sliced asparagus, omitting the tips.

Melt the remaining butter in a frying pan (skillet) large enough to hold all the eggs. When the butter is hot but not brown, pour in the beaten eggs. Use a fork to scrape any egg sticking to the side of the pan towards the middle. Continue to cook until the omelette reaches the right consistency. Fold the omelette and place on a warmed serving dish. Arrange the asparagus tips around, sprinkle with chives and serve.

I never want anything again for our dinners, except what we've heard cried in the street. It's such fun. And to think that we shall have to wait two whole months before we hear: "Green and tender beans, fresh green beans!" How true that is: tender beans; you know I like them as soft as soft, dripping with oil and vinegar, you wouldn't think you were eating them, they melt in the mouth like drops of dew. (The Captive)

French bean salad

Ingredients: 1¼ lb/600 g/1¼ lb good-quality French beans, 6 oz/175 g/6 oz ripe but firm tomatoes, a selection of various salad leaves, 2 oz/50 g/4 tbsp chopped shallots, salt. *Vinaigrette:* 6 tbsp/90 ml/9 tbsp olive oil, 1 tbsp/15 ml/1½ tbsp wine vinegar, 1 tbsp/15 ml/1½ tbsp mustard, juice of ½ lemon, 1 tbsp/15 ml/1½ tbsp chopped broad-leaved parsley, ½ tbsp/7.5 ml/¾ tbsp cut chervil, salt and pepper.

Trim and string French beans and boil in a generous quantity of salted water, uncovered so that the beans retain their color. Cook for 8–12 minutes according to size. When ready, rinse under cold running water to stop cooking and refresh them, then drain.

Prepare the vinaigrette by mixing together the above ingredients. Wash, skin and seed the tomatoes, then dice the flesh. Wash the salad greens and dry in a salad-spinner. Toss the beans, tomato and shallot together in the vinaigrette.

Arrange a bed of salad greens on each of four plates, and place the French bean salad on top. Serve cold or lukewarm.

"It's not a Japanese salad, is it?" she said in a loud undertone, turning towards Odette. (Swann in Love)

Annette:

The potatoes must be boiled in broth, then cut in thin slices as for any other salad; while they are still luke-warm, you season them with salt, pepper, very good olive oil, vinegar.

Henri:

Tarragon vinegar?

Annette:

Orléans is better, but it is not very important, the great thing is half a glass of white wine – Château Yquem, if possible; many herbs cut very small. Cook meanwhile very large mussels au court bouillon with a head of celery, let them drain well, and add them to the seasoned potatoes. Mix the whole lightly and delicately. (...) When the salad is finished, mixed...

Henri:

Delicately.

Annette:

You cover it with rounds of truffles, a real calotte de savant.

Henri:

Cooked in champagne?

Annette:

That's a matter of course. All these preparations two hours before dinner. The salad must be quite cold when served.

(Alexandre Dumas fils, Francillon, Act I, Scene II)

Japanese salad

Ingredients: 1¾ lb/800 g/1¾ lb small new potatoes, 1¾ pints/1 litre/1 quart mussels, 5 tbsp/75 ml/7½ tbsp sweet white wine (for example, Sauternes), 1 celery stick, 7 oz/200 g/7 oz *crosnes* or Chinese artichokes (or Jerusalem artichokes), salt, 1 tsp/5 ml/1 tsp chopped truffle (optional). *Vinaigrette:* 5 tbsp/75 ml/7½ tbsp olive oil, 2 tbsp/30 ml/3 tbsp white wine vinegar, 1 tbsp/15 ml/1½ tbsp chopped broad-leaved parsley, 1 tbsp/15 ml/1½ tbsp chopped chives, 1 tbsp/15 ml/1½ tbsp cut chervil, salt and pepper.

Wash the potatoes, place in cold salted water and bring to the boil. After about 20 minutes test with the point of a knife. Drain.

Clean the mussels very carefully one by one. Scrape and remove "beards", and discard any mussels that gape or stay open after being tapped sharply. Wash under running water (they should not be left in water). Place in a large, broad-based pan with the white wine and celery stick, and boil on a high heat until open, stirring from time to time. As soon as they open, remove the pan from the heat and leave to cool slightly. Shell the mussels, discarding any that have remained closed, and reserve the liquid.

Prepare the vinaigrette by mixing all the ingredients together.

To clean the Chinese artichokes, wrap them in a thick cloth with cooking salt and rub with the palms of the hands. This will remove the fine film which covers them. Cut the ends off. (If using Jerusalem artichokes, scrub them well.) Boil in salted water for about 15 minutes. Test to see that they are done, then drain through a colander and cool under cold running water. (Remove the skin from the Jerusalem artichokes.)

Skin the potatoes and cut into ¼ inch/5 mm slices. Place the Chinese artichokes and mussels in a salad bowl and mix gently.

Serve salad on four plates and arrange the potatoes on top. Dress with the vinaigrette. Chopped truffles may be added to the salad, which can be served warm or cold.

...*Jean who, with his mind set on baked eggs and filet béarnaise, was beginning to think that the velvety heads of the purple irises on the surface of the water and the fragrant scent of Syrian roses at the corners of the path provided insufficient provender for an appetite sharpened by a morning's work, the passage of time and greed.* (Jean Santeuil)

Baked eggs

Ingredients: 8 new-laid eggs, 1½ oz/40 g/3 tbsp butter, salt and white pepper, 16 fl oz/475 ml/2 cups *crème fraîche.*

Preheat the oven to 375°F/190°C/gas mark 5. Butter and season four medium ramekins. Break 2 eggs into each, taking care not to damage the yolks. Place the ramekins in a large ovenproof dish filled with hot water, which should reach halfway up the ramekins. Bake for 8–10 minutes in the oven in the bain-marie (water bath). The whites should be set and the yolk still soft. Cover the eggs with foil for the final 5 or so minutes. Remember that the heat from the ramekins will continue to cook the eggs between oven and table.

Meanwhile reduce the *crème fraîche* by half over a low heat until it thickens and will coat a wooden spoon. Season with salt and pepper.

As soon as the eggs are removed from the oven pour a little reduced cream around the yolks and serve immediately.

"If when you look at a Chardin you can say to yourself, this is intimate, is comfortable, is alive like a kitchen, when you walk about a kitchen you will say to yourself, this is interesting, this is grand, this is beautiful like a Chardin."
Jean Baptiste Chardin, The Jar of Olives, Louvre, Paris.

This little group in the Balbec hotel looked at each new arrival with suspicion, and, while affecting to take not the least interest in him, hastened, all of them, to interrogate their friend the head waiter about him (...) and their lady-wives, having heard that his wife was "expecting," would sit after meals working each at one of the "tiny garments," stopping only to put up their glasses and stare at my grandmother and myself because we were eating hard-boiled eggs in salad, which was considered common and was "not done" in the best society of Alençon. (Within a Budding Grove)

Egg, tomato, anchovy and tuna salad

Ingredients: 6 new-laid eggs, a little vinegar, 4 medium ripe tomatoes, 4½ oz/120 g/4½ oz lambs' lettuce (corn salad), 1 heart of curly endive, 3 oz/75 g/½ cup chopped shallots, a small bunch of chives, chopped, 2 tbsp/30 ml/ 3 tbsp chopped broad-leaved parsley, 9 oz/250 g/9 oz canned tuna in brine, 8 anchovy fillets. *Vinaigrette:* 6 tbsp/90 ml/9 tbsp peanut oil, 2 tbsp/30 ml/3 tbsp old red wine vinegar, 1 tsp/5 ml/1 tsp mustard, salt and pepper.

Using a slotted spoon, place the eggs in a saucepan of boiling water with a few drops of vinegar. Bring the water to the boil again and cook the eggs for 8–10 minutes according to size. Drain and cool.

Prepare the vinaigrette by mixing all the ingredients together. Remove the tomato stalks, and place the tomatoes first in boiling water for about 30 seconds, then in cold. Skin, cut into six wedges and seed. Wash the lamb's lettuce and curly endive, discarding any damaged leaves. Dry in a salad spinner. Mix the salad leaves with the shallots, herbs and tuna and add the vinaigrette. Shell the eggs and cut into four.

"The Ambassador," my mother told her, "assured me that he knows nowhere where one can get cold beef and soufflés as good as yours." Françoise, with an air of modesty and of paying just homage to the truth, agreed, but seemed not at all impressed by the title "Ambassador"; she said of M. de Norpois, with the friendliness due to a man who had taken her for a chef: "He's a good old soul, like me." (Within a Budding Grove)

Cheese soufflé

Ingredients: 6 fl oz/75 ml/¾ cup milk, 2 fl oz/50 ml/¼ cup single cream, ¾ oz/20 g/1½ tbsp butter, ¾ oz/20 g/1½ tbsp flour, 3 egg yolks, 5 egg whites, 3 oz/75 g/¾ cup grated Gruyère cheese, freshly grated nutmeg, salt and pepper.

Preheat the oven to 400°F/200°C/gas mark 6. Boil the milk, cream and grated nutmeg (to taste) in a saucepan. Melt the butter in another saucepan. Add the flour to the butter and cook for 4–5 minutes, stirring constantly. Add the boiling milk and cream mixture to this roux and stir briskly to avoid lumps for 4 minutes. Stir in the cheese. Remove from the heat and add the egg yolks one by one, stirring constantly. Season with salt and pepper.

Use a little extra butter and flour to coat a 6 inch/15 cm soufflé dish, turning the dish to ensure that the sides are well coated with flour. Beat the egg whites with a pinch of salt until stiff but not dry. Stir a tablespoon of white into the

cream mixture first, then gently fold the remainder in.

Pour into the soufflé dish and smooth the surface. Bake for about 25 minutes until well risen, but not too dry, and serve immediately. (Or cook for less time if you like a very moist interior to the soufflé.)

"I would stop by the table, where the kitchen-maid had shelled them, to inspect the platoons of peas, drawn up in ranks and numbered, like little green marbles, ready for a game."

FISH

"But we don't suppose for a moment that you're exaggerating. We only want you to go on with your dinner, and my husband too. Give M. Biche some more sole, can't you see his has got cold? We're not in any hurry; you're dashing round as if the house was on fire. Wait a little; don't serve the salad just yet." (Swann's Way)

Sole in sea-food sauce

Ingrédients: 4 sole, each weighing about 9 oz/250 g/9 oz, 5½ oz/160 g/5½ oz smelts, 18 oz/500 g/18 oz mussels, 12 oysters, 4½ oz/120 g/1 cup shelled prawns or shrimps, 12 button mushrooms, 1 oz/25 g/2 tbsp butter, juice of 1 lemon, 2 oz/50 g/½ cup chopped shallots, 2 oz/50 g/½ cup dried breadcrumbs, oil for frying, 5 tbsp/75 ml/7½ tbsp Calvados, 8 fl oz/250 ml/1 cup single cream, 2 fl oz/50 ml/¼ cup double cream, 2 egg yolks (optional), salt and pepper. *Fumet (fish stock):* 18 oz/500 g/18 oz whiting or sole bones, 1 tbsp/15 ml/1½ tbsp olive oil, 2 oz/50 g/½ cup chopped carrots, 2 oz/50 g/½ cup chopped onions, 17 fl oz/500 ml/a good 2 cups dry white wine, 1 *bouquet garni.*

Ask your fishmonger to gut the sole and clean the smelts. For the stock ask the fishmonger for fish bones. Soak the whiting bones for several hours in cold water, then drain well.

Heat the olive oil in a saucepan, and when hot, add the carrots and onions. Cook, uncovered, on a low flame for 5 minutes. Add the fish bones, cook for 4–5 minutes, then pour in the wine. Boil to reduce slightly, then add 17 fl oz/500 ml/a good 2 cups water and the *bouquet garni.* Bring to the boil and simmer on a low flame for 40 minutes. Skim the froth from the surface. Strain the stock through a fine sieve. Leave to one side.

Wipe the mushrooms and dry them with a clean cloth. Cut into quarters and sauté briefly in a third of the butter with a quarter of the lemon juice (reserve the cooking juices). Open the oysters and reserve their juices. Clean the mussels (see page 138), and place over a high flame to open. Remove from shells and reserve their juices.

Preheat oven to 400°F/200°C/gas mark 6. Season the fish with salt and pepper. Melt the remaining butter in an oven-proof pan, add the shallots and place the sole on top. Add about 12 fl oz/350 ml/1½ cups of the fish stock, and bring to the boil. Cover the pan and place in the oven for about 15 minutes. Meanwhile, roll the smelts in breadcrumbs, fry in a little oil over medium heat, and drain.

Remove the sole from the oven and keep warm. Strain the fish liquor into a saucepan, add the Calvados, and boil to reduce a little. Add the oyster water, about 4 fl oz/120 ml/½ cup mussel juices, and the mushroom juice, and boil to reduce by half. Add the creams and simmer on a low flame, stirring constantly, until the sauce begins to thicken. Once it has the right consistency, add the mushrooms, mussels, prawns, shrimps and oysters, and heat through. If the sauce is too thin, it can be thickened with the beaten egg yolks, but it must not be allowed to boil.

Arrange the sole on hot serving plates and pour over the sauce. The smelts should be seasoned with salt and served separately at the last minute.

Serving suggestion: Serve with boiled or steamed rice.

The sun is beating down. A breeze blows off the lake. My boat is ready. I am leaving you to get some fresh air and fish for trout before dinner. I shall think of you during those exquisite moments... (Marcel Proust's letters, 1893)

Trout with almonds

Ingredients: 4 trout, each weighing about 7 oz/200 g/7 oz, 2 oz/50 g/½ cup flour, 3 tbsp/45 ml/4½ tbsp ground-nut oil, 4 oz/100 g/½ cup butter, 2¼ oz/60 g/½ cup slivered almonds, juice of 1 lemon, salt and pepper, 1½ oz/40 g/3 tbsp chopped parsley.

Ask your fishmonger to clean the trout. Wash thoroughly under running water to remove all traces of blood from the insides. Dry with a clean cloth.

Flour the fish on both sides, then hold each fish up by the tail and tap gently to remove excess. Season with salt and pepper. Heat the oil and 1½ oz/40 g/3 tbsp of the butter in a large frying pan. When hot, fry the trout for about 5 minutes on each side. Remove from the pan and place on a hot serving dish.

Discard the fat and wipe the pan clean with absorbent paper. Melt the remaining butter in the pan and add the almonds. Shake the pan continually, and remove from the heat when the almonds are golden brown. Add lemon juice and sprinkle this basic sauce over the fish. Garnish with chopped parsley and serve.

For upon the permanent foundation of eggs, cutlets, potatoes, preserves, and biscuits, which she no longer even bothered to announce, Françoise would add – as the labour of fields and orchards, the harvest of the tides, the luck of the markets, the kindness of neighbours, and her own genius might provide, so that our bill of fare, (…) reflected to some extent the rhythm of the seasons and the incidents of daily life – a brill because the fish-woman had guaranteed its freshness, a turkey because she had seen a beauty in the market at Roussainville-le-Pin, cardoons with marrow because she had never done them for us in that way before (…). (Swann's Way)

Brill braised in cider

Ingredients: 1 brill, weighing about 4½ lb/2 kg/4½ lb, 5 green apples, 4 oz/100 g/½ cup butter, 4 oz/100 g/2 cups chopped button mushrooms, 4 oz/100 g/1 cup chopped white of leeks, 2 oz/50 g/½ cup chopped shallots, 17 fl oz/500 ml/a good 2 cups cider, 1 tbsp/15 ml/1½ tbsp cider vinegar, salt, 1 tbsp/15 ml/1½ tbsp chopped chives.

Ask your fishmonger to fillet the brill. Core, chop and liquidize the apples without peeling them.

Melt 1 oz/25 g/2 tbsp of the butter in a saucepan. Add the chopped mushrooms, leeks and shallots and fry gently until lightly browned. Add the cider and liquidized apple. Bring to the boil then place the brill fillets in the saucepan. Season with salt, cover and cook for 5 minutes over a low heat. Preheat the oven to 400°F/200°C/gas mark 6.

Carefully transfer the fish fillets to an ovenproof dish and cover with damp absorbent paper. Stir the sauce left in the pan and push through a fine sieve into a small, heavy-based saucepan. Reduce over a low heat until it reaches the consistency of a light purée. Cut the remaining butter into small pieces. Add to the purée and beat over a low heat until it thickens. Check seasoning and add the cider vinegar. Continue to beat.

Reheat the brill fillets in the oven, briefly still with the paper on top so that the fish does not become dry. Arrange the fillets on four warm plates, pour over the sauce and garnish with the chopped chives.

Serving suggestion: Small boiled or steamed potatoes or fresh baby asparagus can be arranged around the fish. You may prefer to use small shelled crawfish tails or scampi.

"Here is the menu. As a first course there is red mullet. Shall we try them?"

"I shall, but you are not allowed them. Ask for a risotto instead. But they don't know how to cook it."

"Never mind. Waiter, some mullet for Madame and a risotto for me." (The Fugitive)

Grilled red mullet

Ingredients: 4 red mullet, each weighing around 7 oz/200 g/7 oz, 5 tbsp/75 ml/7½ tbsp olive oil, salt and pepper, 1 tbsp/15 ml/1½ tbsp chopped broad-leaved parsley. *Niçoise sauce:* 4½ oz/120 g/4½ oz ripe tomatoes, 2 oz/50 g/⅓ cup black olives, ¾ oz/20 g/1 tbsp drained capers, ⅓ oz/10 g/½ tbsp anchovies, 1 tbsp/15 ml/1½ tbsp olive oil, 2 oz/50 g/½ cup chopped shallots, 1 garlic clove, 1 bay leaf, 1 sprig thyme, salt and pepper.

Ask your fishmonger to fillet the red mullet. If you have the patience, use tweezers to remove all the bones. Wrap the fillets in a cloth and refrigerate.

To make the sauce, skin, seed and dice the tomatoes. Stone (pit) the olives. Chop the capers, olives and anchovies together. Heat the olive oil, fry the shallots until lightly browned, then add the chopped caper mixture, garlic, bay leaf and thyme. Season with salt and pepper, mix thoroughly and cook for 30 minutes. Remove and discard the garlic clove, bay leaf and thyme. Keep the sauce warm.

Preheat the grill to its highest setting. Dip the fish fillets into a dish containing a little olive oil, and season with salt and pepper. Place the skin side nearest the hot grill for 1 minute, then turn and grill for a further minute. Place in a hot ovenproof dish.

Working quickly, divide the Niçoise sauce between four plates, garnish with a little chopped parsley and place the fish fillets on top. Pour a few drops of olive oil over the fish and serve immediately.

We had turned into the drive of La Raspelière, where M. Verdurin stood waiting for us on the steps. "I did well to put on a dinner-jacket," he said, observing with pleasure that the faithful had put on theirs, "since I have such smart gentlemen in my party." And as I apologized for not having changed: "Why, that's quite all right. We're all friends here. I should be delighted to offer you one of my own dinner-jackets, but it wouldn't fit you." (...) "Come along, my dear Brichot, get your things off quickly. We have a bouillabaisse which mustn't be kept waiting." (Cities of the Plain)

Bouillabaisse
Fish soup

Ingredients: 4½ lb/2 kg/4½ lb fish pieces (scorpion fish, gurnard, angler fish or monkfish, wrasse or parrot fish, John Dory), 2¼ lb/1 kg/2¼ lb conger eel, 2 whiting, 17 fl oz/500 ml/2¼ cups mussels, 9 oz/250 g/9 oz onions, ½ leek (white part only), 1 stick celery, 1 fennel bulb, 2 large tomatoes, 4 garlic cloves, 6 fl oz/175 ml/¾ cup olive oil, 4 pinches of saffron, 1 pinch of dried savory, a good pinch of dried orange zest, 2 tbsp/30 ml/3 tbsp Pastis, 1 tbsp/15 ml/1½ tbsp chopped broad-leaved parsley, salt and pepper. *Rouille:* 2 inches/5 cm piece of a *baguette*, 4 garlic cloves, 1 red pepper, 1 egg yolk, 6 tbsp/90 ml/9 tbp olive oil.

Ask your fishmonger for pieces of conger eel cut from near the head. There are too many bones at the tail end. Trim, clean, scale and wash all the fish. Clean the mussels (see page 138). Peel and roughly chop the vegetables, seeding the tomatoes. Chop the garlic finely.

Heat half the olive oil in a large pot and gently brown the onions, leeks, celery, fennel, tomatoes and garlic. Add the conger eel and the rest of the fish, apart from the whiting and mussels. Shake the pot in order to mix the ingredients. Add 5½ pints/3 litres/2¾ quarts boiling water or fish stock, and bring to the boil. Add the saffron, savory and orange zest. After 10 minutes add the mussels and whiting and cook for a further 5–7 minutes. A minute or so before the cooking is finished, add the Pastis, parsley and remaining olive oil. Return to the boil and stir to blend in the oil. Season to taste. Discard any unopened mussels.

To make the *rouille*, soak the bread in water, then squeeze as dry as possible. Peel the garlic, removing any shoots. Wash, dry and seed the pepper. Grind the garlic and pepper together in a blender, then tip the resultant purée into a large, deep bowl. Add the crumbled bread and the egg yolk. Beat the mixture as for mayonnaise, adding the olive oil drop by drop.

Float the garlic croûtons spread with the *rouille* in the hot soup.

But above you hangs a strange monster, still fresh like the sea through which it undulated, a ray, the sight of which combines, with gluttonous desire, the curious attraction of the sea, in calm or in storm, of which it was once the fearsome witness, causing as it were a memory from the Zoo to pass through a flavour from a restaurant. It has been laid open and you can admire the beauty of its huge yet delicate architecture, tinged with red blood, with blue nerves and with white muscles, like the nave of a polychrome cathedral. (Against Sainte-Beuve)

Skate in black butter

Ingredients: 3 lb/1.4 kg/3 lb skate, 1¾ lb/800 g/1¾ lb small new potatoes, 1 bay leaf, 1 sprig of thyme, 3 tbsp/45 ml/4½ tbsp white wine vinegar, 4 oz/100 g/½ cup butter, juice of 1 lemon, salt, ⅓ oz/10 g/½ tbsp chopped broad-leaved parsley.

Immerse the skate in cold water, then hold under running water to remove the sticky film covering the fish. Scrub and/or peel the potatoes. Place in a saucepan of cold salted water, and bring to the boil. Cook, covered, for 15 minutes. (They should not be too well cooked, you want to leave them in the hot water until ready to serve.)

Meanwhile place the skate in a large shallow pan. Cover with salted water (½ oz/15 g/½ oz cooking salt to 1¾ pints/1 litre/1 quart water), and add the bay leaf, thyme and vinegar. Bring to the boil, uncovered, on a low heat and simmer for about 15 minutes. Remove the skate, drain and remove the skin using the blunt edge of a knife in order not to damage the flesh.

Divide into four portions using the backbone as a guide. Arrange on four warm plates, surrounded by the drained potatoes, and keep warm. Heat the butter in a frying pan until it turns brown. At the last minute, stir in the lemon juice and some salt. Sprinkle the chopped parsley over each portion of fish, followed by the 'black' butter, and serve immediately.

"What, are you still talking about Dechambre?" said M. Verdurin, who had gone on ahead of us (...) "Listen," he said to Brichot, "don't let's exaggerate. The fact of his being dead is no excuse for making him out a genius, which he was not. He played well, I admit, but the main thing was that he was in the right surroundings here; transplanted, he ceased to exist. My wife was infatuated with him and made his reputation. You know what she's like. I will go further: in the interest of his own reputation he died at the right moment, à point, as the lobsters, grilled according to Pampille's incomparable recipe, are going to be, I hope (unless you keep us standing here all night with your jeremiads in this kasbah exposed to all the winds of heaven)." (Cities of the Plain)

Grilled crawfish in white sauce

Ingredients: 2 live crawfish or rock lobsters, each weighing about 2¼ lb/1 kg/2¼ lb, 2 oz/50 g/4 tbsp lightly salted butter. *Sauce:* 2 chopped shallots, 7 fl oz/200 ml/a scant cup dry white wine, 14 fl oz/400 ml/1¾ cups single cream, ½ tbsp/7.5 ml/¾ tbsp chopped tarragon, 2 oz/50 g/4 tbsp lightly salted butter, salt and pepper, Cayenne pepper.

Place one of the crawfish on a large chopping board, keeping the tail flat, and kill it by banging down with a heavy knife or cleaver where head meets body. Use a large knife to cut it in half lengthways. Remove and discard the stomach sac. Remove the intestines and any coral, and reserve in a small bowl.

Repeat the process with the second crawfish.

To prepare the sauce, place the shallots and white wine in a saucepan and boil to reduce by about a quarter over a high heat, stirring with a wooden spoon. Add the cream and chopped tarragon. Lower the heat and simmer gently until the sauce thickens slightly, stirring occasionally. Mix the butter with the coral and intestines. When the sauce has reached the correct consistency, beat in the butter mixture. Cook for 4–5 minutes, then push through a fine sieve. Check the seasoning and stir in a little Cayenne pepper. Keep warm.

Preheat the grill to its highest setting. Place the crawfish, flesh side upwards, on a baking tray, and dot with the butter. Put the baking tray as far away from the heat as possible, and grill for 7–8 minutes. If the crawfish are not yet golden brown, move the baking tray nearer the heat and continue to grill until golden.

"...he died at the right moment, *à point*, as the lobsters, grilled according to Pampille's incomparable recipe, are going to be..."

Arrange half a crawfish on each plate and serve the sauce, which should be very hot, in a warm sauce boat.

Serving suggestion: If you prefer to flambé the crawfish, heat a little Cognac in a saucepan, set light to it and pour over each fish half.

How could I ever dream again of her dining-room as of an inconceivable place, when I could not make the least movement in my mind without crossing the path of that inextinguishable ray cast backwards ad infinitum, into my own most distant past, by the lobster à l'Américaine which I had just been eating. (Within a Budding Grove)

Lobster American style

Ingredients: 2 live lobsters, each weighing around 1¾ lb/800 g/1¾ lb, 1 tbsp/15 ml/1½ tbsp olive oil, 7 oz/200 g/7 oz fresh tomatoes, 2 garlic cloves, 4 oz/100 g/½ cup lightly salted butter, 4 oz/100 g/1 cup chopped onions, 2 oz/50 g/½ cup chopped shallots, 5 tbsp/75 ml/7½ tbsp Cognac, ½ pint/300 ml/1¼ cups *fumet* (fish stock, see page 142), 1 tbsp/15 ml/1½ tbsp chopped broad-leaved parsley, 1 tsp/5 ml/1 tsp cut chervil, 1 sprig thyme, 1 bay leaf, 1 tsp/5 ml/1 tsp chopped tarragon, salt and pepper.

Kill the lobsters as described in the previous recipe. Cut them in half, clean, then divide into three or four pieces. Break off the claws and crush lightly. Remove and sieve the creamy contents of the head.

Heat the oil in a large heavy-based pan. Fry the pieces of the body for 5 minutes, the head and claws for 10 minutes. The shells should turn red. Drain over the pan and set aside.

Skin, seed and dice the tomatoes. Peel and chop the garlic. Melt half of the butter in the pan and fry the chopped onions, shallots and garlic until lightly browned, stirring from time to time. Flambé with the Cognac, then add the diced tomatoes, the *fumet*, parsley, chervil, thyme and bay leaf. Season with a pinch of freshly ground pepper and a pinch of Cayenne pepper. Bring to the boil and simmer gently for about 15 minutes. Add the creamy contents of the head. Check seasoning. Add the remaining butter and the tarragon (chopped at the last minute), and stir the sauce constantly with a wooden spoon until it thickens.

Add the lobster pieces to the sauce, (you could sieve this first, although it is not strictly necessary). Remove the thyme and bay leaf. Heat through for 3 minutes, but do not allow to boil. Serve on a warm serving dish with boiled rice.

"There are baked eggs for lunch today, filet of beef with béarnaise sauce and fried potatoes. Do you like filet béarnaise?" – *"I should think I do, Uncle!"* – *"Good: and there may be gudgeon, too, if old David has brought any – but I can't be sure about that. Good heavens! It's a quarter past eleven, time to be getting home if we don't want the fry to be spoiled!"* (Jean Santeuil)

Fried gudgeon

Ingredients: 2¼ lb/1 kg/2¼ lb small gudgeon (or smelts or whitebait), 4 oz/100 g/1 cup flour, 3½ fl oz/100 ml/⅓ cup groundnut oil, salt and pepper, 1 bunch of parsley.

Heat the groundnut oil in a deep frying pan. Season and lightly flour the fish, then fry them in the boiling oil for 1–2 minutes according to size. Drain immediately on absorbent paper.

Wash and dry the parsley. Deep-fry for 15 seconds and leave to drain on absorbent paper. Sprinkle on the fried fish and serve immediately.

(...) And by a mechanical contraption which was worked by one of Monsieur Santeuil's father's horses and forced water up from the canal below where Jean, taking care to sit in the shade so as not to be seen by the fish, played his line for great carp which he soon had lying beside him on the grass among the buttercups at a spot where the swans, by reason of the lattice-work hanging from the rustic bridge, could not come. (Jean Santeuil)

Carp with tomato

Ingredients: 2 carp, each weighing 1¾ lb/800 g/1¾ lb, 1 tbsp/15 ml/1½ tbsp olive oil, 14 oz/400 g/3 cups chopped onions, ⅓ oz/10 g/½ tbsp chopped almonds, a handful of wash sultanas, 1 tsp/5 ml/1 tsp salt, a few peppercorns. *Tomato sauce:* 6 good-sized ripe tomatoes, 1 onion, 1 garlic clove, 1 tbsp/15 ml/1½ tbsp olive oil, 1 sprig thyme, 1 bay leaf.

Ask your fishmonger to skin and fillet the carp. To make the tomato sauce, skin and coarsely chop the tomatoes. Peel and chop the onion and garlic. Heat the olive oil in a deep frying pan and gently brown the garlic, chopped onion, thyme and bay leaf. Add the tomatoes and continue to fry over a low heat until all the liquid has evaporated. Keep warm.

Heat the olive oil in a saucepan large enough to hold the carp fillets without overlapping. Gently fry the chopped onions until lightly browned, then add the chopped almonds and sultanas. Stir in salt and peppercorns, then add the carp fillets. Cover them with cold water and place a clean cloth over the pan so that it touches the stock (this ensures that the fish will cook evenly). Cook for 15 minutes. Remove the fillets and keep warm.

Strain the cooking liquid through a fine sieve before adding the onion, sultana and almond mixture to a little of it for the sauce.

Divide the carp fillets into four equal portions.

Check the seasoning of the tomato sauce and arrange on four warm plates. Arrange the fish on top and pour over the almond and sultana sauce.

"A dinner which was infinitely better and more enjoyable than usual ... and it would be difficult to say whether it was the brightness of the light shed by the second lamp which had been added that day, the fried gudgeons served as an entrée, or the warmth that came from being nearer the fire, that most contributed to the pleasure and enjoyment of the occasion."

The Villebon side was completely different. One of its charms was that the Loire river was always in evidence. The first time was on leaving the village, when it could be crossed by an ancient wooden bridge (not much more than a plank with a rope on one side only as a parapet). At the end of this bridge was a plum tree, in summer covered with bluish leaves, and under the plum tree was a fisherman wearing a straw hat and an alpaca jacket who also seemed to have sprouted from that very spot with the onset of the warm weather. Every now and again, a carp came to the surface of the Loire, gaping with hunger or restlessness, giving a sort of protracted sigh of irritation and yearning for what lay beyond. (Swann's Way)

Carp in beer

Ingredients: 4 carp fillets, each weighing about 5–7 oz/150–200 g/5–7 oz, 3 oz/75 g/6 tbsp butter, 4 oz/100 g/1 cup chopped onions, 3 oz/75 g/¾ cup chopped celery, 8 fl oz/250 ml/1 cup beer, 8 fl oz/250 ml/1 cup *fumet* (fish stock, see page 142), 2 oz/50 g/1 cup diced good gingerbread, salt and pepper.

Melt half the butter in a deep frying pan (skillet). Gently fry the chopped onions and celery for about 5 minutes without browning. Add the beer and bring to the boil, then add the *fumet* and return to the boil. Add the gingerbread and lay the carp fillets on top. Season with salt and pepper, cover and cook on a low heat for about 5 minutes (cooking time depends on the thickness of the fillets). When cooked, arrange on a warm serving dish.

Push the sauce through a fine sieve and boil until reduced by half. Check the seasoning, add the remaining butter and beat to give a little more volume. Pour the sauce over the carp fillets before serving.

And it is a delight to the imagination of the eye and also, I am not afraid to say it, of what used to be called the gullet, to see a brill placed before us which has nothing in common with those anything but fresh brills that are served at the most luxurious tables, which in the slow course of their journey from the sea have had the pattern of their bones imprinted upon their backs; a brill that is served not with the sticky paste prepared under the name of white sauce by so many chefs in great houses, but with a genuine white sauce, made with butter that costs five francs a pound... (Time Regained)

Brill with white sauce

Ingredients: 4 brill fillets, each weighing about 5–7 oz/150–200 g/5–7 oz, 2 oz/50 g/4 tbsp butter, 2 oz/50 g/½ cup chopped shallots, 3 tbsp/45 ml/4½ tbsp double cream, 1¼ oz/30 g/¼ cup flour, juice of ½ lemon, salt and pepper.

Melt half the butter in a large saucepan and gently fry the chopped shallots for 2 minutes. Add 8 fl oz/250 ml/1 cup cold water, bring to the boil then add the cream. Bring back to the boil. Place the brill fillets in the pan and season with salt and pepper. Cover and cook over a low heat for about 5 minutes (cooking time depends on the thickness of the fillets).

Meanwhile, soften the remaining butter and blend into the flour with a fork. Remove the brill fillets from the pan, arrange on a serving dish and keep warm.

Bring the fish liquor to the boil. Add the butter and flour blend (*beurre manié*) and whisk until the sauce thickens slightly. Check the seasoning and stir in the lemon juice. Pour the sauce over the fish fillets and serve immediately.

Serving suggestion: Serve with plain boiled rice or pasta.

For Mamma and Françoise, Saturday was important for another reason; it was at the Saturday morning "council" that the menu for the family dinner on Sunday evening was decided. The proposal of a choice turbot, which we had not eaten for a long time, supported by the fact that the latter was very fine indeed and that my uncle was very partial to it, was offset by the proposal of a partridge with cabbage. The fact that my father had to go out after dinner, which meant that this dish would not lay as heavy on his stomach as usual was a point in its favour. (Swann's Way)

Grilled turbot with hollandaise sauce

Ingredients: 4 turbot steaks, each weighing 9 oz/250 g/9 oz, 2 oz/50 g/⅓ cup flour, 3 tbsp/45 ml/4½ tbsp olive oil, 8 sprigs of parsley, salt and pepper, hollandaise sauce to serve (see right).

Preheat the oven to 350°F/180°C/gas mark 4. Heat the grill to its highest setting (a top-heat grill or stove-top grill). Season the turbot steaks with salt and pepper and lightly coat with flour.

Brush the grill rack or stove-top grill with oil and arrange the fish steaks diagonally across it. After 1 minute, turn the steaks by 90 degrees in order to achieve a criss-cross pattern on the surface. Grill for 1 more minute. Turn the steaks over and repeat the process. When the fish has been grilled for 2 minutes each side, place in an ovenproof dish and set to one side.

Make the hollandaise sauce (see right). When it is ready, place the turbot steaks in the oven and bake for 4–5 minutes until cooked through.

Arrange each steak on a warmed plate with the parsley. Serve with the hollandaise sauce.

Serving suggestion: Steamed potatoes go well with this dish.

Hollandaise sauce

Ingredients: 1 chopped shallot, 5 tbsp/75 ml/7½ tbsp dry white wine, juice of ½ lemon, 7 oz/200 g/a scant cup clarified butter (see below), 3 new-laid egg yolks, salt and white pepper, Cayenne pepper (optional).

Place the chopped shallot, white wine and lemon juice in a small, heavy-based frying pan and cook, uncovered, until the liquid has reduced by two-thirds. Allow to cool.

Melt the butter over a low heat.

Add the egg yolks to the pan containing the shallot mixture then place in a hot bain-marie (water bath). Over a very gentle heat stir with a wire whisk, "attacking" the sides and bottom of the pan using wide, sweeping movements. The sauce has reached the right consistency when it forms a "ribbon" as it runs off the whisk. Remove from the heat and carefully add the melted butter, a little at a time. Whisk continually until all the butter has been added. Season with salt and pepper, adding a pinch of Cayenne pepper if you like.

Strain the sauce through a fine sieve and serve in a warmed sauce boat.

Clarified butter

Melt your chosen amount of butter very slowly in a heavy-based saucepan until froth forms on the surface. This normally takes around 20 minutes. Remove the pan from the heat and use a slotted spoon to skim off the top brown froth. Strain the butter through a cloth or filter paper into a storage container. All the impurities will be removed. Keep refrigerated.

The cakes and tarts "...reminded me of those cake-plates with the Arabian Nights pattern, the subjects on which so diverted my aunt Léonie when Françoise brought her up, one day Aladdin and his Wonderful Lamp, another day Ali-Baba, or the Sleeper Awakes or Sinbad the Sailor embarking at Bassorah with all his treasures."

(Overleaf) Sinbad the Sailor plate, Musée de la faïence, Montereau; King Dadbin plate, Servoise collection, Paris.

... A band of red sky above the sea, compact and clear-cut as a layer of aspic over meat, then, a little later, over a sea already cold and steel-blue like a grey mullet, a sky of the same pink as the salmon that we should presently be ordering at Rivebelle, reawakened my pleasure in dressing to go out to dinner. (Within a Budding Grove)

Grey mullet with cucumber

Ingredients: 2 grey mullet, each weighing about 1¾ lb/ 800 g/1¾ lb, 1 large cucumber. *Court bouillon:* 1 large carrot, 1 large onion, 3 tbsp/45 ml/4½ tbsp white wine vinegar, 1 sprig of thyme, 1 bay leaf, salt. *Sauce:* 1 egg yolk, 4½ fl oz/125 ml/a good ½ cup olive oil, juice of 1 lemon, 1 tbsp/15 ml/1½ tbsp *crème fraîche*, salt and pepper.

Ask your fishmonger to clean and gut the fish. A few hours in advance cut the cucumber into thin slivers, sprinkle with salt, and leave to drain in a colander. Separate the slices with a fork, drain well and pat dry with a clean cloth.

Make the *court-bouillon*. Peel, wash and cut the carrot into rounds. Peel and finely chop the onion. Place in a fish kettle with 3½ pints/2 litres/2 quarts water, the vinegar, thyme and bay leaf, and salt to taste. Simmer gently for about 20 minutes.

Place the mullet in the *court-bouillon* and poach very gently for 20 minutes. Remove the fish from the liquid, drain and fillet. Keep warm.

While the fish is cooking, prepare the sauce. Whisk the egg yolk with the oil (as for mayonnaise), and season with salt and pepper. Add the lemon juice and *crème fraîche* (if the sauce curdles, add a spoonful of very cold water and continue to add some oil). Check the seasoning.

Mix the cucumber slices with a little of the sauce. Arrange them on the side of each plate, using a fork to lift them and give a little more volume. Serve the fillets of fish alongside, coated with the sauce.

And a fish poached in court-bouillon was brought in on a long earthenware platter, on which, standing out in relief on a bed of bluish herbs, intact but still contorted from having been dropped alive into boiling water, surrounded by a ring of satellite shell-fish, of animalcules, crabs, shrimps and mussels, it had the appearance of a ceramic dish by Bernard Palissy. (The Guermantes Way)

Poached bass

Ingredients: 1 bass, weighing 2–2½ lb/1–1.25 kg/2–2½ lb, juice of ½ lemon, 11 oz/300 g/a scant 1½ cups butter, salt and pepper. *Court-bouillon:* 1¾ pints/1 litre/1 quart white wine, 1¾ pints/1 litre/1 quart water, 2 finely chopped onions, 1½ oz/40 g/½ cup chopped parsley stalks, a sprig of thyme, 1 bay leaf, salt and coarsely ground pepper.

Ask your fishmonger to clean and gut the fish. Mix all the *court-bouillon* ingredients in a pan (large enough to hold the whole bass) and bring to the boil. Lower the heat and leave to simmer gently for half an hour. Allow to cool.

Place the fish in the cold *court-bouillon*, bring slowly to the boil and simmer for about 30 minutes.

While the bass is cooking, prepare the sauce. Put 2 tbsp water, a pinch of salt, a little pepper and the lemon juice in a small saucepan. Bring to the boil, then reduce the heat and add the butter, a knob at a time, moving the pan to melt it, rather than stirring. The sauce should not separate and the butter should have a thick, milky consistency (it must be

served immediately).

When the bass is cooked, remove from the pan, and place carefully on a cloth to drain thoroughly. Arrange on a dish, and serve with the butter sauce in a sauce boat.

"a fish poached in court-bouillon was brought in on a long earthenware platter (...) it had the appearance of a ceramic dish by Bernard Palissy."

MEAT

...The big hanging lamp, ignorant of Golo and Bluebeard but well acquainted with my family and the dish of stewed beef, shed the same light as on every other evening. (Swann's Way)

For instance, today some beggar of a chef sent me up a leg of mutton with béarnaise sauce – it was done to a turn, I must admit, but just for that very reason I took so much of it that it's still lying on my stomach. (The Guermantes Way)

Casserole of beef

Ingredients: 2¼ lb/1 kg/2¼ lb chuck steak, 1 oz/25 g/1 oz piece of streaky bacon, 1½ lb/700 g/1½ lb carrots, 7 oz/200 g/1½ cups chopped onions, 17 fl oz/500 ml/a good 2 cups dry white wine, 1 *bouquet garni*, 10 peppercorns, salt, 1 oz/25 g/½ cup chopped parsley.

Ask your butcher to cut the meat into 3 oz/75 g/3 oz pieces.

Fry the bacon over a high heat in a large casserole to brown on all sides. Drain, then brown the meat in the bacon fat. Remove from the casserole. Preheat the oven to 350°F/180°C/gas mark 4.

Peel and finely dice a third of the carrots, and fry with the chopped onion in the bacon fat until lightly browned. Add the white wine, bring to the boil and add the *bouquet garni*. Return the meat to the casserole, along with the peppercorns. Add enough water to cover the meat, then bring to the boil and place in the oven for about 3 hours.

Peel and wash the remaining carrots and slice into rounds about ¼ inch/5 mm thick. When the meat has cooked for 3 hours, remove it from the casserole and transfer to another. Strain the meat juices and vegetables in a fine sieve and add the juices to the meat with the sliced carrots. Check the seasoning, stir, cover and place in the oven for a further hour.

Serve the beef in a warm serving dish surrounded by the carrots and sprinkled with chopped parsley.

Leg of lamb with béarnaise sauce

Ingredients: 1 leg of lamb, weighing about 5¼ lb/2.4 kg/5¼ lb, 3 onions, 2 tbsp/30 ml/3 tbsp olive oil, 3 oz/75 g/6 tbsp butter, 1 garlic bulb, 1 tsp/5 ml/1 tsp chopped fresh thyme, 2 bay leaves, salt and pepper, 7 oz/200 g/1 cup béarnaise sauce (see overleaf).

Preheat the oven to 425°F/220°C/gas mark 7. Peel the onions and slice into six wedges. Grease a large roasting tin with the olive oil and heat in the oven. Season the lamb with salt and pepper, then brown in the hot pan.

When well browned, dot with the butter, and arrange the onion wedges, the head of garlic cut in two, the thyme and bay leaves around the joint. Bake in the oven for 55 minutes (or longer if you prefer it less rare). If the onions start to burn during cooking add a small glass of water.

When the joint is cooked, remove from the oven and leave to stand for 30 minutes. This will make the meat more tender. To keep it warm, wrap the meat in foil, or put in the oven for 3–4 minutes before serving. Carve and serve immediately with béarnaise sauce.

Serving suggestion: The meat can be served with sauté potatoes or with French beans sautéed in butter.

Béarnaise sauce

Ingredients: 7 oz/200 g/a scant cup clarified butter (see page 151), 2 fl oz/50 ml/¼ cup white wine vinegar, 1 tsp/ 5 ml/1 tsp coarsely ground pepper, 1¼ oz/30 g/3 tbsp chopped shallots, 1 heaped tbsp/15–20 ml/1½–1¾ tbsp chopped tarragon, 3 egg yolks, 1 tsp/5 ml/1 tsp cut chervil, salt, Cayenne pepper.

Slowly melt the clarified butter.

Place the vinegar, coarsely ground pepper, chopped shallots, and most of the chopped tarragon in a high-sided frying pan (skillet). Reduce by a quarter over a high heat. Leave to cool.

Add the egg yolks to the cooled mixture, then add 3 tbsp/ 45 ml/4½ tbsp cold water. Beat rapidly with a wire whisk over a very low heat, gradually turning up the heat so that the sauce cooks very slowly. Remove from the heat when the sauce achieves a rich, creamy consistency. Pour in the melted butter very slowly and gradually, stirring constantly.

Press the sauce through a fine sieve with the back of a spoon. Season with salt, 1–2 pinches of Cayenne pepper and the remaining herbs.

Keep the béarnaise sauce in a bain-marie (water bath) until ready for use.

It seemed quite natural, therefore, to send for him whenever a recipe for some special sauce or for a pineapple salad was needed for one of our big dinner-parties, to which he himself would not be invited. (...) this early Swann abounding in leisure, fragrant with the scent of the great chestnut-tree, of baskets of raspberries and of a sprig of tarragon. (Swann's Way)

Sauce gribiche

Ingredients: 6 eggs, 2 tsp/10 ml/2 tsp mustard, 17 fl oz/ 500 ml/a good 2 cups groundnut oil, 2 oz/50 g/½ cup chopped gherkins (dill pickles), 1 tbsp/15 ml/1½ tbsp chopped parsley, ½ tbsp/7.5 ml/¾ tbsp each of chopped chives and chervil, 1 tsp/5 ml/1 tsp chopped tarragon, ¼ pint/150 ml/a good ½ cup white wine vinegar, 1½ oz/40 g/ 1½ oz drained capers, salt and pepper.

Hard-boil the eggs and allow to cool. Mash the egg yolks with the mustard to a smooth paste in a large, deep bowl. Add the oil, drop by drop, as for mayonnaise. Chop the egg whites and mix ino the egg yolk sauce base along with the gherkins (dill pickles), aromatic herbs, vinegar and capers. Season with salt and pepper.

Serving suggestion: Sauce gribiche goes well with cold meat or fish.

She had gone herself to the Halles to procure the best cuts of rump-steak, shin of beef, calves' feet, just as Michelangelo spent eight months in the mountains of Carrara choosing the most perfect blocks of marble. (Within a Budding Grove)

Jellied beef

Ingredients: 2¼ lb/1 kg/2¼ lb silverside beef, larded (see below), 2 oz/50 g/¼ cup bacon fat, 1 calf's foot, 7 oz/200 g/ 7 oz small onions, 7 oz/200 g/7 oz young carrots, ¾ oz/ 20 g/1½ tbsp butter, 4 egg whites, salt. *Marinade:* 2½ pints/1.5 litres/6¼ cups red wine, 4 fl oz/120 ml/½ cup brandy, 7 oz/200 g/1½ cups sliced or diced carrots, 7 oz/ 200 g/1½ cups finely chopped onions, 2 bay leaves, 2 sprigs of thyme, 2 sprigs of parsley.

The day before, ask your butcher to lard the joint with pieces of salted and unsalted bacon and then to tie it up.

To make the marinade, pour about 4 fl oz/120 ml/1½ cups of the red wine and half of the brandy into a large pot. Add all the other ingredients and stir. Place the meat in the marinade, cover the pot with cling film (food wrap) and refrigerate for 12 hours.

When you want to cook, preheat the oven to 350°F/180°C/gas mark 4. Drain the joint well, holding it over the marinade pot. Melt the bacon fat in a large, deep roasting tin and, when hot, brown the meat on all sides. Pour over the remaining brandy and flambé. Add the remaining red wine and boil to reduce by a quarter. Add the marinade and its vegetables to the roasting tin and top up with water so that the meat is completely covered.

Put the calf's foot in cold water for 5 minutes, then drain and add to the meat. Bring to the boil, then add salt sparingly (remember that the beef is partly larded with salt bacon). Cover and bake in the oven for at least 3 hours.

Peel the small onions and trim and scrub the carrots. Remove the cooked meat from the oven, but keep the oven hot. Strain the meat juices through a fine sieve. Wipe the roasting tin with absorbent paper, then melt the butter in it. Add the onions and carrots and cook until lightly browned. Add the strained meat juices to the pan, place the meat in the middle, cover and bake for a further hour. When the meat is completely cooked, reserve.

Strain the pan juices through a fine sieve into a saucepan, and bring to the boil. Beat the egg whites and add them to the boiling liquid in order to clarify it (the impurities will cling to the egg whites). Bring back to the boil and simmer gently for 5 minutes. Strain through a sieve lined with a fine cloth.

Untie the meat, and carve into ¼ inch/5 mm slices. Arrange the slices in a deep serving dish with the carrots and onions on top. Pour enough pan juices in, (these will form the jelly), to reach half-way up the meat, and refrigerate for at least 3 hours.

And overnight Françoise had sent to be cooked in the baker's oven protected with breadcrumbs, like a block of pink marble packed in sawdust, what she called a "Nev'-York ham." Believing the language to be less rich in words than it is, and her own ears untrustworthy, the first time she had heard someone mention York ham she had thought, no doubt, – feeling it to be hardly conceivable that the dictionary could be so prodigal as to include at once a "York" and a "New York" – that she had misheard, and that the ham was really called by the name already familiar to her. (Within a Budding Grove)

Baked York ham

Ingredients: **1 whole lightly cured ham, 14 fl oz/400 ml/1¾ cups Madeira, cornflour (if necessary), salt and pepper.**

Before beginning this recipe, soak the ham in cold water for 6 hours.

Place the ham in a stewing pan and cover with fresh cold water. Bring to the boil, skim and leave to simmer gently. Allow 20 minutes' cooking time for each 1 lb/450 g of meat.

Half an hour before cooking is completed, remove the ham from the stock, (retain this), peel away the skin and trim off any surplus fat. Preheat the oven to 325°F/160°C/gas mark 3.

Place the ham in a braising pan with the Madeira, cover with a tight-fitting lid and bake in the oven for 1 hour.

For the sauce, boil the cooking stock to reduce it by three-quarters. Add 7 fl oz/200 ml/a scant cup of it to the ham, and Madeira, and cook for 15 minutes over a low heat (if the sauce is too thin, you can thicken it slightly with a little cornflour). Season to taste.

Carve the ham, coat with the sauce and serve immediately.

Serving suggestion: If you want to display and serve the ham on the bone, you can glaze it. To do this, coat the ham with the Madeira sauce and put in a very hot oven just long enough for the sauce to caramelize on the ham.

In a butcher's shop, between an aureole of sunshine on the left and a whole ox suspended from a hook on the right, a young assistant, very tall and slender, with fair hair and a long neck emerging from a sky-blue collar, was displaying a lightning speed and a religious conscientiousness in putting on one side the most exquisite fillets of beef, on the other the coarsest parts of the rump (...) although he did nothing afterwards but arrange in the window a display of kidneys, steaks and ribs – was really far more reminiscent of a handsome angel who, on the Day of Judgment, will organize for God, according to their quality, the separation of the good and the wicked and the weighing of souls. (The Captive)

Calves' kidneys cooked in Cognac

Ingredients: 3 choice, pale calves' kidneys, 6 oz/175 g/¾ cup butter, 2 oz/50 g/¼ cup chopped shallots, ¼ pint/150 ml/¾ cup Cognac, 7 fl oz/200 ml/a scant cup single cream, juice of ¼ lemon, 1 tbsp/15 ml/1½ tbsp Dijon mustard, 7 oz/ 200 g/4 cups sliced button mushrooms, 1 tbsp/15 ml/1½ tbsp chopped broad-leaved parsley, salt and pepper.

Preheat the oven to 375°F/190°C/gas mark 5. Select a cast-iron casserole with enough room to lay the kidneys side by side. Remove the transparent membrane surrounding the kidneys. Melt 2 oz/50 g/¼ cup of the butter in the casserole and fry the kidneys over a brisk heat until brown, then put in the oven for 14 minutes. The kidneys are now cooked. Place them in a dish and cover with another dish.

Remove the fat from the casserole, and fry the shallots gently without letting them brown. Add the cognac and simmer the liquid to reduce by three quarters, then add the cream; simmer to reduce by half.

Cut 3 oz/75 g/6 tbsp of the remaining butter into small pieces and add gradually to the mixture, stirring constantly. Add the lemon juice and the mustard. Blend into the sauce but do not bring back to the boil. Add seasoning to taste.

Wipe, dry and thinly slice the mushrooms, then sauté them in the remaining butter. Add them to the sauce. Cut the kidneys into thin strips and gently mix into the sauce with their juices. Sprinkle with the chopped parsley and a pinch of coarsely-ground pepper. Heat but do not allow to boil. Arrange the kidneys in their sauce on four hot plates. Serve immediately.

"I should be interested to see how your chef managed a dish of quite a different kind; I should like, for instance, to see him tackle a boeuf Stroganoff." (Within a Budding Grove)

Boeuf Stroganoff

Ingredients: 1½ lb/700 g/1½ lb fillet of beef, 3 oz/75 g/ 6 tbsp butter, 3 tbsp/45 ml/4½ tbsp groundnut oil, 5 oz/ 150 g/1 cup chopped onions, 4 fl oz/120 ml/½ cup white wine, 14 fl oz/400 ml/1¾ cups single cream, 1½ beef stock cubes, paprika, salt and pepper.

Cut the meat into thick strips, approximately ¾ inch/1.5 cm wide and 1½ inches/4 cm long. Season with salt and a little paprika.

Heat half the butter and the oil in a frying pan. When the butter has turned a deep golden colour, fry the meat quickly to seal it so the outside is browned and the inside is still rare. Remove from the heat and set aside on a plate.

Wipe the frying pan clean of fat, heat it again, then gently fry the onions for 3–4 minutes without letting them brown. Add the white wine and simmer to reduce by half; add the single cream, the crumbled stock cubes and 2 small pinches of paprika. Stir, cook and thicken over a low heat.

When the sauce is smooth, add the remaining butter, stirring continuously. Add the meat to the sauce, season to taste and serve immediately.

Serving suggestion: Serve with plain boiled rice.

"Here is the carcass of an ox ... these are not so much things that Rembrandt painted as the representation of Rembrandt's own taste, those ideas which are part of every great man..." The Slaughtered Ox, Rembrandt Van Rijn, Louvre, Paris.

Early in the morning, before we were dressed, without rhyme or reason, save for the pleasure of proving the strength of our solidarity, we would call to one another good-humouredly, cordially, patriotically, "Hurry up, there's no time to waste; don't forget it's Saturday!" while my aunt, conferring with Françoise and reflecting that the day would be even longer than usual, would say, "You might cook them a nice bit of veal, seeing that it's Saturday." (Swann's Way)

Casserole of veal

Ingredients: 2¼ lb/1 kg/2¼ lb joint of veal (topside or cushion, or rump), 2 oz/50 g/2 oz smoked streaky bacon rashers, 4 large firm potatoes, 3 large onions, 3 garlic cloves, 3 tbsp/45 ml/4½ tbsp groundnut oil, 1 sprig thyme, 2 bay leaves, 2 oz/50 g/4 tbsp butter, salt and pepper.

Preheat the oven to 350°F/180°C/gas mark 4. Wrap the rashers of streaky bacon around the joint, tying them on with string. Season with salt and pepper. Peel, wash and dry the potatoes and quarter them; peel the onions and cut each into six; peel the garlic.

Heat the oil in a casserole over a brisk heat, put in the joint and fry until evenly browned, then remove. Drain the fat from the casserole and add the onions, garlic, thyme and bay leaves. Fry for 1 minute over a medium heat. Lay the joint on top of this mixture, dot with the butter, cover and put in the oven for 45 minutes.

After the joint has been cooking for 15 minutes, arrange the potatoes around it, then continue cooking. If the onions are becoming too dark, add a glass of hot water to the casserole. If necessary, repeat this procedure.

Remove the string, carve the joint and serve hot, surrounded by the vegetables.

Serving suggestion: You can also serve a mixed green salad with it.

... A spiced beef in which the aspic doesn't taste of glue and the beef has caught the flavour of the carrots. (Within a Budding Grove)

Beef braised in wine

Ingredients: 2¼ lb/1 kg/2¼ lb good braising steak, 2½ pints/1.5 litres/6¼ cups red wine, 11 oz/300 g/11 oz unsmoked streaky bacon rashers, 18 oz/500 g/18 oz carrots, 7 oz/200 g/7 oz onions, 4 oz/100 g/4 oz button mushrooms, 4 oz/100 g/4 oz tomatoes, ½ garlic bulb, 1 *bouquet garni*, salt and pepper.

The day before, ask your butcher to cut the meat into chunks, each weighing approximately 3 oz/75 g. Cover the meat with the red wine, season sparingly, cover the bowl and refrigerate.

The next day, line the sides and bottom of an earthenware dish or a casserole with the rashers of streaky bacon.

Scrub, trim and dry the carrots; chop them into ¼ inch/5 mm slices. Peel the onions and slice them thinly. Wipe and dry the mushrooms, then slice. Skin the tomatoes, seed and quarter. Peel the garlic, clove by clove.

Cover the bottom of the dish with a bed of some of the carrots, onions and mushrooms. Drain the meat, reserving the marinade, and place on top of the vegetables. Add the remaining vegetables together with the tomatoes, the garlic cloves and the *bouquet garni*. Season and then pour in the marinade. Top up with water so that the liquid just covers the meat. Cover and put in the oven for about 4 hours.

Serving suggestion: Fresh pasta goes well with a daube.

Then there was a dish called la petite marmite. The first time he mentioned it I didn't know what it was. And although he knew what it tasted like, he was just as ignorant as I was about the recipe.

"I don't really know how to describe it," he said. "I think you have to mix special bits of beef with chicken gizzards and many other little things. And it has to simmer for a very long time on a low flame. But it's delicious." (Céleste Albaret, Monsieur Proust)

Meat and vegetable broth

Ingredients: 2¼ lb/1 kg/2¼ lb good braising steak in the piece, 3¼ lb/1.5 kg/3¼ lb top ribs or knuckle of beef (with bone), 2 beef stock cubes, 4 marrow bones, 7 oz/200 g/7 oz carrots, 5 oz/150 g/5 oz turnips, 5 oz/150 g/5 oz celery sticks, 7 oz/200 g/7 oz baby leeks, 12 baby onions, 8 chicken wings, groundnut oil, 7 oz/200 g/7 oz green cabbage or kale leaves, 20 slices of French bread, salt and pepper, grated Gruyère cheese.

Place the pieces of beef in a large stewing pan, and cover with cold water. Add a pinch of salt and bring to the boil. Skim off any scum and fat, then crumble in the stock cubes.

Leave the marrow bones under running water to flush out the blood. Trim, scrub and cut the carrots, turnips and celery into chunks. Wash and slice the white part of the leeks into chunks. Peel the baby onions and fry them with the chicken wings in a little hot oil. When they are well browned, remove from the heat and add, with the vegetables (apart from the cabbage or kale) to the pan containing the meat. Bring to the boil and leave to cook over a low heat for 2 hours.

To prepare the kale, remove the outer stalks and any withered leaves. Wash the leaves which are to be used and leave them in a saucepan of boiling salted water for 5 minutes. Then rinse in cold running water, drain and reserve.

Remove the turnip chunks from the broth after they have been cooking for 2 hours, otherwise their flavour will be too overpowering. Also move the leeks which may disintegrate if left. (When cool, cut both into julienne strips.) Add the cabbage or kale to the pan and cook for another hour. Add the marrow bones 30 minutes before the end of cooking.

Check that the meat is cooked through. If it is, take out the vegetables, cut into strips (apart from the onions), and divide between four small earthenware "marmite" dishes, adding several strips of the reserved turnips and leek to each one. Remove the marrow bones.

Make small balls with the kale leaves. To do this, put a large kale leaf into the middle of a clean cloth. Holding the four corners of the cloth, twist them round as if wringing, until all the water has dripped out and the kale has formed a tight ball. Add these balls to the marmites with the chicken wings and a small quantity of each different meat. Strain the broth into a saucepan through a sieve lined with muslin; the broth should be clear and a rich maroon color. Bring to the boil, season to taste, and fill the marmites with the broth.

Toast the slices of bread, spread each one with a little marrow, and float on the surface of the broth in each marmite. Sprinkle the marrow with a pinch of ground pepper. Serve piping hot, accompanied by grated cheese in small dishes.

GAME AND POULTRY

"We must hurry back because we're having those lovely hares you sent, for luncheon: they were beginning to smell delicious when I came away." (Jean Santeuil)

Jugged hare

Ingredients: 1 medium hare, 2 tbsp/30 ml/3 tbsp vinegar, 7 oz/200 g/7 oz lean bacon, 2 garlic cloves, 20 small pickling onions, 4 oz/100 g/½ cup butter, 7 oz/200 g/1½ cups finely chopped onions, beer, 2 tbsp/30 g/3 tbsp flour, 3½ pints/2 litres/2 quarts red wine, 1 *bouquet garni*, 20 small button mushrooms, 4 slices white sandwich bread, the hare's liver, salt and pepper, 3 oz/75 g/½ cup chopped parsley. *Marinade:* 2 tbsp/30 ml/3 tbsp Cognac, 2 tbsp/30 ml/3 tbsp olive oil, 4 oz/100 g/¾ cup finely chopped onions, salt and pepper.

The day before, skin and gut the hare and cut into portions. Reserve the liver and the blood in a bowl with the vinegar to prevent the blood from coagulating. Refrigerate. Put all the ingredients for the marinade and the pieces of hare into a large basin, and add salt and pepper. Cover and leave to marinate overnight in the refrigerator. Turn the pieces of hare occasionally.

The next day, cut off the bacon rind and cut the bacon into strips or lardons. Put these in a saucepan and cover with cold water. Bring to the boil and cook for 4 minutes over a very low heat. Rinse the bacon in cold running water and dry in a clean cloth. Peel the garlic and the small pickling onions.

Melt 1 oz/25 g/2 tbsp of the butter in a casserole and, when hot, fry the diced bacon in it, stirring continuously. When it is nicely browned, remove the bacon and fry the (drained and wiped) pieces of hare on each side. When they have turned a golden brown color, remove them. Then gently fry the onions, using a little beer to help brown. Add the flour and stir to make a blond roux. Dilute with the red wine, bring to the boil and add the garlic and the *bouquet garni*. Put all the ingredients back into the liquid in the casserole and season with salt and pepper. Cover and cook over a low heat for about an hour.

Meanwhile, gently fry the small pickling onions in a knob of the remaining butter until they are lightly browned. After wiping and drying the mushrooms, sauté them in a little more butter; when they are cooked, remove them and add the juices to the casserole. Lightly fry the bread cut into 8 triangles in the remaining hot butter over a low heat.

Remove, then sauté the hare's liver and cut into four thin slices. Put to one side. When the hare is cooked, remove the pieces, and put them in a saucepan with the baby onions and mushrooms.

Bring the sauce in the casserole to the boil. Remove from the heat and pour in the blood, beating to ensure that the mixture blends perfectly. Strain the sauce over the meat in the saucepan using a fine sieve, and gently reheat (but do not allow to boil). Arrange the meat, vegetables and sauce on a hot serving dish, and garnish with the slices of fried bread. Top with the slices of liver and the chopped parsley.

Serving suggestion: Jugged hare can be served with fresh pasta or a celery gratin.

"Seeing that he has confided to you the secrets he has got from them, they will no longer be chary of confiding them to you themselves. Still life above all will become animate. Like life itself, it will always have something new to say to you, some wonder to make to shine, some mystery to reveal; everyday life will delight you, if for a few days you have have harkened to its depiction as to a lesson; and from having grasped that life in its depiction, you will have gained the beauty of life itself." (Against Sainte-Beuve)

Jean Baptiste Chardin, Dead Rabbit with Partridge, Musée de la Chasse et de la Nature, Paris.

For I had extorted from Françoise, who though a pacifist was cruel, a promise that she would cause no undue suffering to the rabbit which she had to kill, and I had had no report yet of its death. Françoise assured me that it had passed away as peacefully as could be desired, and very swiftly. "I've never seen a beast like it; it died without saying a blessed word; you would have thought it was dumb." (Within a Budding Grove)

Rabbit with bacon

Ingredients: 1 rabbit, weighing around 2¾ lb/1.3 kg/2¾ lb, 7 oz/200 g/7 oz lightly smoked streaky bacon, 1¼ lb/600 g/1¼ lb firm potatoes, 1 tbsp/15 ml/1½ tbsp olive oil, 5 oz/150 g/1 cup chopped onions, ½ pint/300 ml/1¼ cups dry white wine, salt and pepper, 1 oz/25 g/1 oz chopped parsley.

Ask your poulterer to cut the rabbit into eight pieces. Season the pieces. Dice the bacon, put into a saucepan with some cold water and bring to the boil. After a minute, rinse the bacon in cold water and put to one side. Peel and wipe the potatoes (if you need to wash them, do so quickly without letting them soak in the water). Cut into ¾ inch/2 cm cubes, and reserve wrapped in a clean cloth.

Heat the oil in a casserole. When hot, fry the pieces of rabbit until well browned all over and then remove them. Then fry the diced bacon quickly to seal, remove and drain. Brown the diced potatoes in the casserole, and remove with a slotted spoon to drain. Gently fry the chopped onions, then pour in the white wine. Simmer to reduce until only a quarter of the liquid is left in the casserole.

Add the rabbit pieces and some water, so that the meat is just covered by the liquid. Cover and cook for about 20 minutes over a medium heat. Add the diced potatoes and the bacon. Continue cooking for about another 15 minutes (stir from time to time, but be careful not to crush the potatoes). Check that the rabbit is cooked through, and season to taste.

Arrange the pieces of rabbit on a hot serving dish, coat with the sauce and top with the potatoes. Just before serving, garnish with chopped parsley.

"Saint-Loup with helm of bronze," said Bloch, "have a piece more of this duck with thighs heavy with fat, over which the illustrious sacrificer of birds has poured numerous libations of red wine." (Within a Budding Grove)

Wild duck with cranberries

Ingredients: 2 small wild ducks, 2 oz/50 g/½ cup chopped onions, 1¾ pints/1 litre/1 quart red wine, 1 *bouquet garni*, 3 basil leaves, 1 tbsp/15 ml/1½ tbsp cornflour, 2oz/50 g/½ cup cranberries, a little butter, salt and pepper. *Aromatic sauce base*: 2 oz/50 g/¼ cup sugar, 4 fl oz/120 ml/½ cup white wine vinegar, 1¾ pints/1 litre/1 quart red wine, 20 coriander seeds, 20 peppercorns, 1¼ inch/3 cm piece each of lemon and orange zest, ¼ inch/1 cm cinnamon stick.

Preheat the oven to 350°F/180°C/gas mark 4. To prepare the aromatic sauce (caramel and vinegar) base, slightly brown the sugar in a saucepan, then pour in the vinegar and reduce until the liquid has almost evaporated. Then add the wine, coriander seeds, peppercorns, citrus fruit zest and cinnamon, and reduce again over a low heat until the liquid has almost evaporated.

Carefully pluck, singe and truss the ducks. Season them well with salt and pepper. Heat a flameproof and ovenproof dish over a brisk heat. Put the ducks in, breast side down. When a "crust" has formed, put the dish in the oven for about 10 minutes. Remove the dish from the oven and let the ducks stand for about 20 minutes. Cut the breasts and legs off the carcasses. Keep them hot.

Crush the carcasses and put the duck in the cooking dish with the onions. When they are well browned, pour in the wine. Bring to the boil and add the *bouquet garni* and the basil leaves. Add the aromatic sauce base and cook over a medium heat. The sauce should reduce by half (to leave enough for four people). Thicken with the cornflour blended in a little water. Stir well, then check the seasoning and the tartness. Add the cranberries, a small knob of butter and stir carefully to thicken.

Finish cooking the legs by roasting them in the oven for 15 minutes. Gently reheat the breasts. Carve the breasts on the slant and arrange them on the plates in a fan shape. Coat them with the sauce.

Serve the legs on a bed of green salad after the breasts, or on the same plate as the breasts.

Serving suggestion: The duck can be served with some unsweetened chestnut purée.

When visiting the princesse de Guermantes, the friends of the duchesse appeared somehow different, seen in the company of women with whom I did not usually associate them. Their intimacy with the princesse de Hesse reminded me suddenly of what I had forgotten. Being in the habit of imagining, before going to see the duchesse, the probable attendance of Mme d'Arpajon and Mme de Souvré, envisaging them as an integral and everyday part of dinner, similar to the chicken chasseur or the beef stroganoff, I had forgotten how they acted as the marquise d'Arpajon or the duchesse de Souvré, the roles that their ancestors had played. (Cities of the Plain)

Sautéed chicken

Ingredients: 1 chicken, weighing around 3 lb/1.3 kg/3 lb, 3 oz/75 g/6 tbsp butter, 5 tbsp/75 ml/7½ tbsp groundnut oil, 1 oz/25 g/4 tbsp sliced shallots, 7 oz/200 g/4 cups sliced button mushrooms, 3 tbsp/45 ml/4½ tbsp Cognac, 2 fl oz/50 ml/¼ cup dry white wine, 1 stock cube or 7 fl oz/200 ml/a scant cup veal stock, salt and pepper, ½ tbsp/7.5 ml/¾ tbsp chopped tarragon, ½ tbsp/7.5 ml/¾ tbsp cut chervil.

Ask your poulterer to draw and joint the chicken. Season the pieces with salt and pepper. Preheat the oven to 400°F/200°C/gas mark 6.

Melt 2 oz/50 g/4 tbsp of the butter in a large sauté pan with the oil. When the fat is smoking, add the chicken pieces, skin side down. When they are a nice golden color, turn them and fry the other side. Then put the sauté pan in the oven for 20–25 minutes. To ensure that the larger pieces of chicken are cooked through, pierce them with the point of a knife: if the juice is pinkish, continue cooking for a few more minutes. Then remove the chicken from the pan.

Pour away most of the fat left in the pan, then gently fry the shallots over a very low heat, stirring with a wooden spoon. Add the mushrooms and brown over a brisker heat. Do not cover. When the vegetable juices have evaporated, pour in the Cognac and flambé. Add the white wine, and boil to reduce by three-quarters. Crumble in the stock cube or, preferably, use the veal stock, then season with a little salt and pepper and cook for 4–5 minutes. Add the remaining butter, stirring vigorously. Check the seasoning.

Arrange the chicken pieces on the serving dish and reheat them for several minutes. Just before serving, pour over the sauce. Sprinkle with the finely chopped tarragon and chervil at the last minute to retain their full fragrance.

M. de Guermantes having declared (following upon Elstir's asparagus and those that had just been served after the chicken financière) that green asparagus grown in the open air (...) ought to be eaten with eggs. "One man's meat is another man's poison, as they say," replied M. de Bréauté. "In the province of Canton, in China, the greatest delicacy that can be set before one is a dish of completely rotten ortolan's eggs." (The Guermantes Way)

Fricassee of chicken in Madeira and truffle sauce

Ingredients: 1 chicken, weighing 3¼ lb/1.5 kg/3¼ lb, 4 oz/100 g/4 oz lean ham, 11 oz/300 g/11 oz medium white mushrooms, 4 oz/100 g/½ cup butter, 2 bay leaves, 1 sprig thyme, 1 tsp/5 ml/1 tsp coarsely ground pepper, ½ pint/300 ml/1¼ cups Madeira, 1 beef stock cube or 4 fl oz/120 ml/½ cup veal stock, 4 oz/100 g/4 oz cocks' combs, 4 oz/100 g/4 oz chicken kidneys, 4 slices white sandwich bread, salt and pepper, 2 tsp/10 ml/2 tsp chopped parsley.

Ask your poulterer to divide the chicken into eight pieces. Dice the ham. Salt the chicken on all sides. Wipe and dry the mushrooms, then separate the caps from the stalks.

Heat 1 oz/25 g/2 tbsp of the butter and, when it is hot and has turned a light golden color, seal the pieces of chicken. When they are well browned on all sides, remove and keep to one side. Lightly sauté the mushroom stalks, then add the ham, bay leaves, thyme and pepper. Gently fry, stirring occasionally, then pour in about 4 fl oz/120 ml/½ cup of the Madeira. Reduce, over a low heat, until the liquid has nearly evaporated. Add the stock cube, (dissolved in a little water) or, preferably, the veal stock, then the chicken legs. Cook over a very low heat for 10 minutes, then add the chicken wings.

Meanwhile boil the cocks' combs in salted water, for at least 20 minutes. Rinse them in cold water and dry them. Peel away the membrane surrounding the poultry kidneys. Trim the crusts from each slice of bread and cut each slice into a heart shape. Fry in some of the remaining butter, heated to a nut-brown color.

Fry the mushroom caps in a little more hot butter. Reserve the caps, and pour the liquid into the pan with the chicken pieces. Likewise, fry the kidneys in hot butter, until lightly browned.

Remove the chicken pieces when cooked, and transfer to another pan. Keep warm. Strain the sauce through a fine sieve into a small saucepan and bring to the boil. Season to taste. Add the rest of the Madeira and blend in a knob of butter. Stir. Add the mushroom caps, the cocks' combs and chicken kidneys. Simmer for 10 minutes.

In the centre of each plate, arrange a bread heart topped with a piece of chicken and surrounded by the garnish. Pour over the sauce, and sprinkle with parsley.

We drank Cliquot champagne and ate exquisite partridges, cooked with special care for a friend of the marquis by the cook. (The Guermantes Way)

Partridges with champagne

Ingredients: 4 partridges, 2 oz/50 g/4 tbsp butter, ½ tbsp/7.5 ml/¾ tbsp olive oil, 8 garlic cloves, 4 bay leaves, 4 sprigs of thyme, 4 French bread croûtons, 1 tsp/5 ml/1 tsp chopped parsley, salt and pepper. **Forcemeat:** 1 chopped shallot, a dash of olive oil, the partridge livers, 2 fl oz/50 ml/¼ cup champagne, salt and pepper.

Ask your poulterer to dress the partridges. Season them. Preheat the oven to 425°F/220°C/gas mark 7. Melt half the butter in a sauté pan with the oil, put in the partridges and brown them on all sides. Add the peeled garlic, the bay leaves and the thyme. Put the sauté pan in the oven and cook for 14

minutes. When the partridges are cooked, remove them from the pan and let them rest for 15–20 minutes. Keep the oven at the same temperature. Add a little water to the pan to make a small amount of gravy.

For the forcemeat, gently fry the chopped shallot in the oil in a small frying pan (skillet), then add the livers and the champagne; allow to reduce. When all the liquid has evaporated, chop the mixture very finely and season with salt and pepper.

Edouard Manet, La Botte d'Asperges, Wallraf-Richartz Museum, Cologne.

Butter the four croûtons of French bread and spread them with the hot forcemeat. Sprinkle with parsley. Carve the partridges and, before serving, put them in the oven for 3 minutes. Meanwhile, boil up the gravy, then strain into a hot sauce-boat. Serve the birds with the gravy and the croûtons.

DESSERTS

"What is this prettily colored thing that we're eating?" asked Ski.

"It's called strawberry mousse," said Mme Verdurin.

"But it's ex-qui-site. You ought to open bottles of Château-Margaux, Château-Lafite, port wine."

"I can't tell you how he amuses me, he never drinks anything but water," said Mme Verdurin, seeking to cloak with her delight at this flight of fancy her alarm at the thought of such extravagance. (Cities of the Plain)

Strawberry mousse

Ingredients: 1¼ lb/600 g/4 cups strawberries, 2 gelatine leaves, 5 oz/150 g/⅔ cup caster (superfine) sugar, juice of ½ lemon, 4 egg whites.

Wash and hull the strawberries, then purée them in a liquidizer. Reserve 7 oz/200 g/1 cup of the purée to serve with the mousse. Soak the gelatine in cold water to soften it.

In a saucepan, mix 4 oz/100 g/½ cup of the sugar, the lemon juice and the remaining strawberry purée. Drain the gelatine well and add to the pan. Gently heat the mixture to dissolve the gelatine. Leave to cool.

Beat the egg whites to stiff peaks and then fold in the remaining sugar. Pour the cooled purée onto the egg whites, and carefully fold together.

Pour the mousse into small individual moulds, and allow to set overnight in the refrigerator. Serve chilled with the unsweetened strawberry purée.

In the same way, her love of food was satisfied by the daily, unchanging repetition of a favourite menu; and the anticipation of the same omelette, the same fried potatoes and the same peach compote caused her to conjure up the pleasures to come, hours beforehand. These expectations would have been dashed by the appearance of scrambled eggs, "depriving her of her omelette", or by a portion of cream-cheese which, once seen, would have provoked a fresh attack of melancholy, knowing she would not be able to have the compote now until the following day. (Swann's Way)

Peach compote

Ingredients: 3½ lb/1.6 kg/3½ lb peaches, 5½ oz/160 g/¾ cup caster (superfine) sugar, juice of ½ lemon.

Skin the peaches and stone (pit) them. Cut the flesh into small chunks and put, along with the sugar and the lemon juice into a heavy-based saucepan.

Bring to the boil, then cook over a low heat for 45 minutes, stirring occasionally. The peaches are ready when their juices have evaporated.

Serving suggestion: You can serve this compote with finely chopped fresh mint leaves.

My mother was counting greatly upon the pineapple and truffle salad. (Within a Budding Grove)

Pineapple and truffle salad

Ingredients: 1 fresh pineapple, 1 small fresh truffle, 1 can of truffle juice.

Remove the skin of the pineapple and cut the flesh into thin slices, removing the centres.

Rinse the truffle in cold water, dry and slice thinly.

Interleave the pineapple and truffle slices in a glass salad bowl, and pour in the truffle juice. Cover the bowl with cling film (food wrap). Chill for 2 hours, gently moving the bowl occasionally so that the pineapple absorbs the truffle's delicate aroma.

Sift the flour into a mixing bowl. Dissolve the yeast in the warm milk. Mix the salt, milk and yeast into the flour to form a smooth dough. Shape into a ball, cover with a clean cloth and leave to rise in a warm place for 1½ hours.

Preheat the oven to 425°F/220°C/gas mark 7. Roll the dough out thickly on a well-floured board. Cut into small rounds the size of an egg, shape into small balls and leave to rise at room temperature, until doubled in size.

Melt the butter and brush over the balls of dough. Put into small round, shallow moulds or, failing that, straight on to a baking sheet. Bake in the oven for about 20 minutes, or until golden.

Serving suggestion: At tea-time, serve the muffins hot with unsalted butter or jam.

When she was in a happy mood because she was going to see the Reine Topaze, or when her expression grew serious, worried, petulant because she was afraid of missing the flower-show, or merely of not being in time for tea, with muffins and toast, at the Rue Royale tea-rooms, (...) Swann (...) would feel so distinctly the soul of his mistress rising to the surface of her face that he could not refrain from touching it with his lips. (Swann's Way)

Muffins

Ingredients: 9 oz/250 g/1 ¾ cups flour, ¼ oz/7 g/¼ oz fresh yeast, 2 fl oz/50 ml/¼ cup warm milk, 1 tsp/5 ml/1 tsp salt, 1 oz/25 g/2 tbsp butter.

"They look quite delicious," broke in Mme Cottard. *"In your house, Odette, one is never short of victuals. I have no need to ask to see the trade-mark; I know you get everything from Rebattet. I must say that I am more eclectic. For sweets and cakes and so forth I repair, as often as not, to Bourbonneux. But I agree that they simply don't know what an ice means. Rebattet for everything iced, and syrups and sorbets; they're past masters. As my husband would say, they're the ne plus ultra."* (Within a Budding Grove)

Coffee bavarois

Ingredients: 5 gelatine leaves, ½ pint/300 ml/1¼ cups milk, 14 fl oz/ 400 ml/1¾ cups whipping cream, 4 eggs, 3½ oz/90 g/½ cup caster (superfine) sugar, 3 tbsp/45 ml/ 4½ tbsp coffee essence (extract).

Soak the sheets of gelatine in cold water to soften them before using.

Boil the milk with about 2 fl oz/50 ml/¼ cup of the cream. Separate the eggs, then beat the egg yolks in a bowl with the sugar until the mixture becomes light and frothy. Add the milk and cream mixture, beating vigorously to prevent the eggs from cooking. Pour into a saucepan and cook over a low heat, stirring continuously with a wooden spatula. The custard is cooked when it coats the back of a wooden spoon; this takes about 7 minutes.

Drain the gelatine and add to the custard with the coffee flavouring. Mix well to dissolve the gelatine, then strain through a fine sieve. Pour the mixture into a bowl and allow to cool, stirring occasionally.

Whip the remaining cream to soft peaks, then fold into the mixture in the bowl: this should have cooled but not set. Pour into four moulds of about 4 inches/10 cm in diameter, 3½–4 inches/8–10 cm high. Put in the refrigerator for 1 hour. Turn out just before serving.

Serving suggestion: The bavarois can be served with custard (see p. 185).

The French name "Noël" was, by the way, unknown to Mme Swann and Gilberte, who had substituted for it the English "Christmas," and would speak of nothing but "Christmas pudding," what people had given them as "Christmas presents," of going away – the thought of which maddened me with grief – "for Christmas." Even at home I should have thought it degrading to use the word "Noël" and always said "Christmas," which my father considered extremely silly. (Within a Budding Grove)

Christmas pudding

Ingredients: 4½ oz/125 g/1 cup beef suet, ½ lemon, 4½ oz/125 g/¾ cup sultanas, 4½ oz/125 g/¾ cup dried currants, 4 oz/100 g/¾ cup crystallized (candied) fruit, 1½ oz/40 g/½ cup flaked almonds, 4½ oz/125 g/1 cup breadcrumbs, 1¼ oz/30 g/a good ⅛ cup flour, 1 tsp/5 ml/ 1 tsp ground allspice, 1 tsp/5 ml/1 tsp ground cinnamon, 3 pinches of grated nutmeg, 4 fl oz/120 ml/½ cup milk, 2 eggs, 2 fl oz/50 ml/¼ cup rum, salt.

Shred the beef suet finely. Squeeze the juice from the lemon and remove and finely chop the zest. Rinse the sultanas and currants and dry them carefully. Dice the crystallized (candied) fruit. Mix all the ingredients except the milk, eggs and rum in a bowl. Add a pinch of salt and blend the mixture together with a wooden spoon.

Preheat the oven to 250°F/130°C/gas mark ½. Add the eggs to the bowl, one after the other, and mix well. Pour in the milk and the rum, stirring continuously, to obtain a smooth paste. Line a medium ovenproof terrine with a large sheet of greaseproof (waxed) paper (do not trim off the surplus). Pour the pudding mixture into the terrine, cover with the paper overhanging, and then cook in the oven in a bain-marie (water bath) for 3½ hours.

Remove from the oven and wait until the terrine dish is cool before wrapping the whole dish in foil. Leave to rest in a cool place for at least an hour.

Before serving the pudding, heat through for an hour in the bain-marie (water bath), and at the same oven temperature. Turn out and flambé with a little extra rum or brandy.

"It was definitely a Sunday tart, gazed at with admiration and eaten with relish on those Sunday noons, with the narrow street outside on the same level as the room..."

My friends preferred the sandwiches, and were surprised to see me eat only a single chocolate cake, sugared with gothic tracery, or an apricot tart. This was because, with the sandwiches of cheese or salad, a form of food that was novel to me and was ignorant of the past, I had nothing in common. But the cakes understood, the tarts were talkative. There was in the former an insipid taste of cream, in the latter a fresh taste of fruit which knew all about... (Within a Budding Grove)

Apricot tartlets

Ingredients: Pastry: 4 oz/100 g/½ cup butter, 4½ oz/110 g/ ¾ cup flour, 2 oz/50 g/½ cup icing (confectioners') sugar, 1 egg yolk, ½ vanilla pod (bean), salt. *Compote:* 18 oz/ 500 g/18 oz apricots, 4 oz/100 g/½ cup caster (superfine) sugar. *Filling:* 18 oz/500 g/18 oz apricots, 3 oz/75 g/ 6 tbsp butter, 2½ oz/60 g/a good ½ cup icing (confectioners') sugar.

For the pastry, take the butter out of the refrigerator an hour before using if possible, as it will be easier to work with. Immerse a mixing bowl in boiling water and wipe dry quickly and thoroughly. In it, cream the butter, cut into small pieces, with a wooden spoon until thick and smooth (do not attempt to *heat* the butter as it will melt, which is not desirable). Put the flour on a floured pastry board and make a well in the centre. Fill this well with the creamed butter, sugar, egg yolk, the scraped-out black vanilla seeds, and a pinch of salt dissolved in 1 tbsp/15 ml/1½ tbsp water. Work all these centre ingredients together with the fingertips, gradually drawing in the flour. Shape the pastry into a ball, wrap in kitchen foil and leave to rest in the refrigerator.

For the compote, wash and dry the apricots. Halve and stone (pit) them, then put the halves in a saucepan with the sugar and 5 tbsp/75 ml/7½ tbsp water. Cook over a low heat, stirring occasionally, but do not cover. Allow the liquid to reduce until completely evaporated (about 30 minutes). The apricots dissolve into a rough purée.

Preheat the oven to 350°F/180°C/gas mark 4.

For the filling, wash, dry, halve and stone (pit) the apricots. Arrange the apricot halves side by side in an ovenproof dish. Brush with the melted butter, then dust with the sugar. Put in the oven for about 15 minutes – they should be lightly browned. Remove.

To bake the tartlets, let the pastry come to room temperature. Raise the oven temperature to 400°F/200°C/gas mark 6. Roll the pastry out on a floured board and cut into 4 inch/10 cm rounds. Use these to line some non-stick round moulds. Crimp the edges of the pastry with your fingers. Fill with paper or foil and baking beans. Put in the oven and bake blind for 30 minutes. Cool.

Fill each tartlet with a little of the compote. Cover with the apricot halves arranged in a circle (about six). Dust with a little extra icing (confectioners') sugar, and pour over a little of the apricot cooking juices.

Serving suggestion: These tartlets can be served with a purée of red fruit and vanilla ice-cream.

... Ladies from the neighboring châteaux who set the hens squawking and the gossips staring as they crossed the marketplace on feast-days, when they came to mass "in their turn-outs," and who, on their way home, just after they had emerged from the shadow of the porch where the faithful were scattering the vagrant rubies of the nave as they pushed open the door of the vestibule, did not fail to buy from the pâtissier in the square some of those cakes shaped like towers, which were protected from the sunlight by a blind – "manqués", "sainte-honorés" and "genoa cakes", whose indolent, sugary aroma has remained mingled for me with the bells for high mass and the gaiety of Sundays. (Against Sainte-Beuve)

Sponge cake

Ingredients: 4 oz/100 g/½ cup butter, 6 eggs, 7 oz/200 g/ 1 cup caster (superfine) sugar, 1½ vanilla pods (beans), 5 oz/150 g/1 cup flour, 2 fl oz/50 ml/¼ cup rum, salt.

Preheat the oven to 350°F/180°C/gas mark 4. Melt the butter in a heavy bottomed saucepan. Separate the eggs. Beat the egg yolks in a bowl with the sugar and the scraped-out black vanilla seeds, until the mixture becomes light and frothy. Gradually sprinkle in the flour, mixing continuously with a wooden spoon. Pour in the melted butter along with the rum. Continue beating to obtain a smooth cake mixture.

Whisk the egg whites and a pinch of salt to stiff peaks; gradually and gently fold into the egg yolk mixture.

Grease a 9 inch/22 cm fluted French sponge pan with a little extra butter, pour in the mixture and bake in the oven for about 35 minutes. Check that the cake is cooked through by piercing it with the point of a knife: this should come out clean. Take out of the oven, turn out on to a cake rack and leave to cool.

Serving suggestion: Serve plain or filled with cream or jam.

But since they were having luncheon late, in spite of the fact that the street was beginning to fill with a Sunday crowd, only the large apple tart was served, a tart that looked as yellow as the door of the General Shop on the Square (...). It was definitely a Sunday tart, gazed at with admiration and eaten with relish... (Jean Santeuil)

Apple tart

Ingredients: 7 oz/200 g/7 oz puff pastry, 18 oz/500 g/18 oz tart dessert apples, 2 oz/50 g/4 tbsp butter, 2 oz/50 g/½ cup icing (confectioners') sugar.

Preheat the oven to 400°F/200°C/gas mark 6. Roll the pastry out to a circular shape and use to line a large flan dish. Trim off any surplus pastry, and crimp the edges with your fingers. Peel, core and slice the apples thinly. Lay them over the pastry base, leaving a space of about ⅛ inch/3 mm between the apples and edge of the flan dish. The apple slices should overlap, forming a circle with a rosette in the centre.

Melt the butter, then brush some over the apples. Dust with some of the sugar. Bake in the oven for 30 minutes. Repeat the melted butter-sugar procedure twice during the cooking time. The apples should be a deep golden color and the pastry well cooked.

Serving suggestion: A scoop of vanilla ice-cream goes well with the hot tart. For a traditional apple tart, spread apple compote over the pastry base before adding the fruit (make this as for apricots on page 177).

"...At the Aigneaux farm, they were sure to find Mme Laudet (...) offering to the entranced gaze of a great concourse of people seated round large wooden tables under the apple-trees the spectacle (...) of a superb bosom of green silk trimmed with black braid (...). In just such a manner did Mme Laudet go from table to table, carrying a bowl of milk or a mug of cider, clad in the green dress which was but one among the many flowers in this gay social springtide, of this burgeoning of the happy human throng with its thousand different colors that go by the name of Sunday Best."

Several of the waiters, let loose among the tables, were flying along at full speed, each carrying on his outstretched palm a dish which it seemed to be the object of this kind of race not to let fall. And in fact the chocolate soufflés arrived at their destination unspilled, the potatoes à l'anglaise, in spite of the gallop that must have given them a shaking, arranged as at the start round the Pauillac lamb. (Within a Budding Grove)

Chocolate soufflés

Ingredients: 4½ oz/125 g/4½ oz plain (semisweet) chocolate, 12 fl oz/350 ml/1½ cups milk, 5 oz/150 g/¾ cup butter, 2½ oz/60 g/½ cup flour, 7 oz/200 g/1 cup caster (superfine) sugar, 6 eggs.

Preheat the oven to 400° F/200°C/gas mark 6. Break the chocolate into pieces, put in a saucepan with the milk, and bring gently to the boil. Meanwhile, cream the butter until thick and smooth (see page 177). Mix in the flour and the sugar, using a wooden spatula. Pour the boiling chocolate milk over the mixture, stir and pour back into the saucepan. Bring to the boil. Separate the eggs. Beat the egg yolks in vigorously, one after the other, then leave to cool.

Coat four 4 inch/10 cm ramekins with extra butter, then dust with extra sugar which will adhere to the butter. Shake the ramekins to dislodge any surplus sugar (do not use your fingers). Whip the egg whites to very stiff peaks then gradually and gently fold into the chocolate mixture.

Pour into the ramekins and cook in the oven for 20 minutes. Serve immediately.

I was as little capable of deciding which of them I should prefer to see as if, at the dinner-table, I had been obliged to choose between rice à l'impératrice and the famous cream of chocolate. (Swann's Way)

Rice pudding with fruit

Ingredients: 9 oz/250 g/1¼ cups short-grain rice, 4 oz/100 g/½ cup crystallized (candied) fruit, 3 tbsp/45 ml/4½ tbsp Kirsch, 3 tbsp/45 ml/4½ tbsp Maraschino liqueur, 1¾ pints/1 litre/1 quart milk, 2 oz/50 g/4 tbsp butter, 5 oz/150 g/¾ cup caster (superfine) sugar, salt, 2 oz/50 g/½ cup gooseberry jelly. *Bavarois:* 4 fl oz/120 ml/½ cup *crème fraîche*, 3 gelatine leaves, ½ vanilla pod (bean), 8 fl oz/250 ml/1 cup milk, 1½ oz/40 g/¼ cup caster (super-fine) sugar, 4 egg yolks.

Preheat the oven to 350°F/180°C/gas mark 4. Chill the *crème fraîche*. Soak the gelatine in cold water to soften. Macerate the crystallized (candied) fruit in the Kirsch and Maraschino liqueurs.

Put the rice in a saucepan. Cover liberally with cold water. Bring to the boil and then cook for 10 minutes. Drain the rice in a sieve and rinse in cold water for several minutes.

Boil the milk in an ovenproof dish, then add the butter, the sugar, the salt and the rice. Bring to the boil and cook in the oven for 20 minutes. Take the rice out of the oven and stir with a fork to separate the grains. Leave to cool a little, then stir in the fruit and liqueurs. Meanwhile prepare the bavarois. Split the vanilla pod (bean) in two, and use a knife to remove the black seeds inside. Add them to the milk and bring the mixture to the boil. Mix the sugar and egg yolks in a bowl. Beat vigorously until the mixture becomes light and frothy. Pour the boiling milk gently over the sugar and eggs, and whisk together. Pour the mixture into a heavy-based saucepan and cook over a low heat, stirring continuously with a wooden spoon. The custard is ready when it has thickened slightly (it should not be allowed to boil). Strain through a sieve into a bowl. Drain the gelatine, squeeze it and put in the bowl with the custard. Stir to dissolve the gelatine.

Melt the gooseberry jelly and use to line a 6½ inch/16 cm savarin mould. Put the mould in the refrigerator to settle the jelly.

When the rice is almost cold and the custard is still warm, blend the two together. Take the *crème fraîche* from the refrigerator and whip to soft peaks. Fold into the rice gently, then pour into the jelly-lined savarin mould. Leave to set in the refrigerator for 3 hours before turning out onto a circular serving dish. The rice can be decorated with some extra crystallized (candied) fruit.

... *Raspberries which M. Swann had brought specially, cherries, the first to come from the cherry-tree which had yielded none for the last two years, a cream cheese, of which in those days I was extremely fond, an almond cake because she had ordered one the evening before, a brioche because it was our turn to make them for the church.* (Swann's Way)

Almond cake

Ingredients: 4 oz/100 g/¾ cup blanched almonds, 3 eggs, 3 oz/75 g/½ cup caster (superfine) sugar, a pinch of salt, 1 knob of butter.

Chop the almonds. Separate the eggs. Using a wooden spatula, mix the almonds, sugar and egg yolks in a bowl.

Preheat the oven to 400°F/200°C/gas mark 6. Beat the egg whites with the salt to very stiff peaks then fold gently in to the mixture. Stir a little to aerate the mixture, but not too vigorously.

Butter a 9½ inch/22 cm fluted French sponge pan, pour in

the mixture from the bowl and bake in the oven for about 45 minutes. Check that the cake is cooked through by piercing with the point of a knife: this should come out clean.

Remove from the oven, turn out on to a cake rack and leave to cool.

Serving suggestion: You can serve the cake plain or with coffee-flavoured custard; you can also fill it with chocolate mousse and coat with hot chocolate sauce.

Miniature brioches

Ingredients: ½ oz/15 g/½ oz fresh yeast, 2 tbsp/30 ml/ 3 tbsp milk, 7 oz/200 g/a scant cup butter, 9 oz/250 g/ 1¾ cups flour, 3 eggs, 1 oz/25 g/2 tbsp granulated sugar, ⅛ oz/5 g/⅛ oz salt, 1 egg yolk, 2 oz/50 g/¼ cup brown sugar.

Mix the yeast with the lightly warmed milk. Cream the butter until thick and smooth (see page 177). Place the flour on a floured pastry board and make a well in the centre. Add the yeast and milk mixture, 3 of the eggs, the granulated sugar, creamed butter and salt to this well. Blend the ingredients in the well together with your fingertips, gradually mixing in the flour, to obtain a smooth dough.

Put the dough into a bowl, cover with a clean cloth and leave to rise for 20 minutes at room temperature. When the dough has puffed up, knead again, then shape into a ball in the bowl. Cover with the cloth again and leave to rest for 2 hours in the refrigerator.

Divide the ball of dough into twelve small pieces. Roll these between your palms to shape them into even rounds. Put them in a dish and leave them, again covered by the cloth, for 30 minutes in the refrigerator.

Take the balls of dough out of the refrigerator and leave them for 2 hours at room temperature. Preheat the oven to 400°F/200°C/gas mark 6. Beat the egg yolk with a little water. Brush this over the tops of the balls of dough, then dust each ball with brown sugar. Bake in the oven for 10–15 minutes. Leave the brioches to cool slightly before serving.

... Mme Swann, (...) having shown one of her visitors to the door, came sweeping in a moment later, (...) and would say with an air of astonishment: "I say, that looks good, what you've got there. It makes me quite hungry to see you all eating cake."
(Within a Budding Grove)

Currant cake

Ingredients: 9 oz/250 g/1¾ cups dried currants, 5 oz/150 g/10 tbsp butter, 4½ oz/125 g/¾ cup caster (superfine) sugar, a pinch of salt, 3 eggs, 6 oz/175 g/1¼ cups flour, 1 tsp/5 ml/1 tsp baking powder.

Soak the currants in warm water to soften them. Cream 4½ oz/125 g/9 tbsp of the butter until thick and smooth (see page 177). Mix the creamed butter in a bowl with the sugar and a pinch of salt, then add the eggs, one by one, blending with a wooden spoon. Strain the currants, then dry them in a clean cloth. In a different bowl, mix together the flour, baking powder and currants. Combine the contents of the two bowls, mix well and leave to rest for 30 minutes.

Preheat the oven to 425°F/220°C/gas mark 7. Heat the remaining butter very lightly and, with a brush, use some to butter the inside of a 9 inch/23 cm long cake tin (pan). Line this with greaseproof (waxed) paper: cut the corners so that the paper follows the shape of the tin as closely as possible. Butter the paper as well.

Pour the cake mixture into the cake tin (pan) and put in the oven. Ten minutes later, raise the oven temperature to 350°F/180°C/gas mark 4 and bake for 35–40 minutes. Test that the cake is cooked through by piercing with the point of a knife: this should come out clean, without any trace of cake mixture.

Remove the cake from the oven, leave to cool, then turn out.

Note: If you wish, crystallized (candied) fruit can be added to this recipe: the same or half the weight of the currants.

And suddenly the memory revealed itself. The taste was that of the little piece of madeleine which on Sunday mornings at Combray (because on those mornings I did not go out before mass), when I went to say good morning to her in her bedroom, my aunt Léonie used to give me, dipping it first in her own cup of tea or tisane. (Swann's Way)

Miniature madeleines

Ingredients: 4 oz/100 g/½ cup butter, 2 eggs, 3 oz/75 g/½ cup caster (superfine) sugar, 3½ oz/90 g/¾ cup flour, ¼ oz/10 g/¼ oz clear honey, salt, ¼ oz/10 g/¼ oz icing (confectioners') sugar.

Melt 3½ oz/90 g/7 tbsp of the butter over a low heat, then leave to cool. Beat the eggs, the caster (superfine) sugar and a pinch of salt in a bowl. After 5 minutes, sprinkle in the flour. Stir with a wooden spoon. Blend in the cold melted butter and the honey. Mix well, but not too vigorously. Leave to rest in the refrigerator for an hour, then take out and leave at room temperature for half an hour. Preheat the oven to 425°F/220°C/gas mark 7. Melt the remaining butter and brush over the madeleine moulds before filling them with cake mixture.

Bake in the oven for 5 minutes if using small moulds and 10 minutes for large ones. Allow to cool slightly before serving.

Serving suggestion: Madeleines can be served with many desserts, fruit salad, sorbets or ice-cream.

"Odette poured out Swann's tea, inquired 'Lemon or cream?' and, on his answering 'Cream, please,' said to him with a laugh: 'A cloud!' And as he pronounced it excellent, 'You see, I know just how you like it.' This tea had indeed seemed to Swann, just as it seemed to her, something precious, and love has such a need to find some justification for itself, (...) that when he left her at seven o'clock to go and dress for the evening, all the way home in his brougham, unable to repress the happiness with which the afternoon's adventure had filled him, he kept repeating to himself: 'How nice it would be to have a little woman like that in whose house one could always be certain of finding, what one never can be certain of finding, a really good cup of tea."

A chocolate cream, Françoise's personal inspiration and speciality would be laid before us, light and fleeting as an "occasional" piece of music into which she had poured the whole of her talent. Anyone who refused to partake of it, saying: "No, thank you, I've finished; I'm not hungry any more," would at once have been relegated to the level of those Philistines who, even when an artist makes them a present of one of his works, examines its weight and material, whereas what is of value is the creator's intention and his signature. (Swann's Way)

Chocolate creams

Ingredients: 4 oz/100 g/4 oz plain (semisweet) chocolate, 17 fl oz/500 ml/a good 2 cups milk, 6 eggs, 4 oz/100 g/½ cup caster (superfine) sugar.

Boil the milk, add the pieces of broken chocolate and melt slowly, mixing with a wooden spoon. Separate the eggs. Beat the sugar and the egg yolks together. Preheat the oven to 250°F/130°C/gas mark ½. When the chocolate is completely melted, pour over the eggs and the sugar, mix together quickly and vigorously and strain through a fine sieve. Pour the mixture into 3 inch/7.5 cm ramekins and cook in the oven, in a bain-marie (water bath), for an hour. Leave to cool before serving.

Vanilla or coffee creams
You can use the same recipe to make individual vanilla creams. Replace the chocolate with the black seeds from a vanilla pod (bean). Strain the milk after heating and infusing.

You can also replace the chocolate with 2 tsp/10 ml/2 tsp coarsely ground coffee; the coffee-flavoured milk must be strained before being mixed with the sugar and eggs.

What do I see? A Nesselrode pudding! As well! I declare I shall need a course at Carlsbad after such a Lucullan-feast as this. (Within a Budding Grove)

Chestnut pudding

Ingredients: 4½ oz/125 g/½ cup chestnut purée, 2½ oz/60 g/¼ cup crystallized (candied) fruit, 2½ oz/60 g/½ cup candied orange peel, 4 fl oz/120 ml/½ cup Malaga wine, 2½ oz/60 g/½ cup each of dried currants and sultanas, 1 dessertspoon Maraschino liqueur, 17 fl oz/500 ml/a good 2 cups whipping cream, *marrons glacés* to decorate.
Custard: 17 fl oz/500 ml/a good 2 cups milk, 5 eggs, 4½ oz/125 g/¾ cup granulated sugar.

If you are making the chestnut purée yourself, remember that it must be very smooth. Dice any large pieces of crystallized (candied) fruit and candied orange peel and macerate them in the Malaga wine. Wash the currants and sultanas, then soak them in warm water. When it is time to use them, remember to drain and dry well in a clean cloth.

To make the custard, boil the milk in a heavy-bottomed saucepan. Separate the eggs. Beat the egg yolks and sugar together in a bowl until the mixture becomes light and frothy (about 5 minutes). Pour the boiling milk over this mixture, then return to the saucepan. Blend together over a low heat, using a wooden spoon or spatula to get right to the bottom of the saucepan. After 5 minutes, the custard – which must not be allowed to boil – should have a thick consistency, coating the back of the spoon with a thin film. Strain through a sieve.

Mix the chestnut purée, the Maraschino liqueur and the custard together well, then add the crystallized (candied) fruit, candied orange peel, currants and sultanas. Whip the cream until very firm and fold in carefully. Pour into a 7 inch/18 cm charlotte mould, lined with greaseproof (waxed) paper. Cover the mould with aluminium foil and put in the freezer at least overnight.

Just before serving, turn the pudding out and decorate with *marrons glacés*.

THE PEOPLE

Abert (Monsieur) : 33
Adolphe (oncle) : 52
Aimé : 101
Albaret (Céleste) : 122,
    124–125, 126
Albertine : 122
Albon (duc d') : 86
Amiot (Jules) : 21
Andrée : 112
Arpajon (Madame d') : 92
Basin : 92
Bauldelaire (Charles) : 102
Belmont (Georges) : 124
Benardaky (Marie) : 44
Béraud (Jean) : 118
Boniface : 84
Borda (G. de) : 118
Botticelli (Sandro di
    Mariano Filipepi) : 50
Boutroux (Monsieur) : 75
Bréauté (Hannibal de) : 92
Bréfort (Monsieur) : 86
Breughel (Bruegel Pieter) :
    60
Brichot : 75–76
Brillat-Savarin (Anthelme) :
    21, 76, 122
Caraman-Chimay (Madame
    de) : 100
Castellane (Marquis de) :
    118
Chardin (Jean-Baptiste
    Siméon) : 102, 128
Clermont-Tonnerre (E. de) :
    92
Cottard
    doctor : 68–69, 71
    Madame : 68, 71
Cottin
    Céline : 122, 126
    Nicolas : 122, 124, 126
Crécy (Odette de) : 44, 52,
    68
Crémieux
    Adolphe : 19
    Cousins : 19
David (father) : 21
Dechambre : 75
Doville (doyen of) : 76
Dumas fils (Alexandre) : 68
Elstir : 92, 94, 106, 112
Fitau (Félicie) : 23, 124,
    126
Flaubert (Gustave) : 118

Forcheville : 68, 70
France (Anatole) : 66, 118
Françoise : 23, 28, 30, 33,
    36, 44, 58, 60, 85, 122,
    126, 128–129
Gallou (Ernestine) : 23
Gandara : 118
Georges (oncle) : 19
Gineste (Marie) : 124
Giotto : 28
Goncourt
    Edmond Huot de :
    70–71, 75
    Brothers : 68
Guermantes
    Duc de : 85–86, 92, 94
    Duchesse Oriane de :
    85–86, 90, 92, 94
Hahn (Reynaldo) : 83, 118
Hals (Frans) : 69
Heudicourt (Zénaïde d') :
    94
la Bruyère (Jean de) : 122
Lemaire (Madeleine) : 66,
    70, 83
Léonardo de Vinci : 128
Léonie (Aunt) : 16, 18, 23,
    33, 36, 106
Luxembourg (la princesse
    de) : 108
Manet (Édouard) : 129
Maurice (François) : 38
Michel-Ange (Michelangelo
    Buonarroti) : 61, 128
Monselet (Charles) : 122
Montargis (Charles) : 58–59
Montesquiou-Fezensac
    (comte Robert) : 118
Norpois (Monsieur de) : 92,
    126, 128
Octave (Madame) : 30, 122
Odette : 44–45, 50, 52, 60,
    66, 68, 71
Palissy (Bernard) : 109
Parme (princesse de) : 92,
    94
Patron (le) : 75–76
Patronne (la) : 70–71, 75,
    86
Proust
    Adrien : 19, 21, 118
    Élisabeth : 21, 38
    Louis : 19
Racine (Jean) : 129
Rembrandt (Rembrandt
    Harmenszoon van Rijn) :

47, 69
Ranvoyzé (Madame) : 58
Réveillon
    Duc de : 83–84
    Duchesse de : 83–84
    Henri : 83–84
Rosemonde : 112
Ruskin (John) : 118
Sagan (prince de) : 118
Saint-Loup (Robert de) :
    59–60, 62, 108, 112
Sainte-Beuve (Charles
    Augustin) : 118
Santeuil (Jean) : 21, 23, 33,
    58, 84
Sévigné (Madame de) : 102
Swann
    Charles : 17, 21, 28, 30,
    36, 44, 50, 52, 66,
    68–69–70–71, 90, 92
    Gilberte : 44–45, 47, 50,
    52, 112
    Odette : 44–45, 47, 50,
    52–53, 62, 66.
Torcheux (Virginie) : 19
Turenne (comte Louis de) :
    118
Verdurin
    the coterie : 66
    the : 66, 71, 75, 85
    Madame : 68, 70–71, 75
    the milieu : 71
    Monsieur : 66, 75–76
    the little clan : 66, 70
Ver Meer de Delft (Vermeer
    Jan) : 44
Véronèse (Paolo Caliari) :
    76
Villeparisis (Madeleine de) :
    92, 102, 108, 112
Viradobetski : 71
Wagner (Richard) : 66, 71
Weil
    Adèle : 19
    the cousins : 19
    Jeanne : 29
    Louis : 19, 52, 122
    Nathée : 19
Weinbourg (princesse de) :
    86

THE PLACES

Alençon : 102

Auteuil : 19, 21, 23, 71
Balbec : 76, 100, 102, 106,
    111–112, 124
    Grand-Hotel of :
    100–101–102, 112
Cabourg (Grand Hotel of) :
    100
Combray : 16–17–18–19,
    21, 30, 33, 44, 52,
    60–61, 85, 92, 100, 122,
    126
Doncières : 59–60–61–62
Guermantes : 83, 86, 90
Illiers : 19, 21, 23, 36, 38
Chartres : 19
Loiret (the café of) : 60
Orléans
    Bannier (the suburb) :
    58
    Coligny (the barracks) :
    58
Paris : 19, 23, 44, 52, 58,
    66, 85, 122
    Anjou (road) : 124
    Boulogne (bois de) : 38
    Champes-Élysées
    (gardens) : 44
    Ciro's : 118
    Coucelles (road) : 126
    Hamelin (road) : 38, 122
    Haussmann (boulevard) :
    16, 19, 38, 122, 126
    Larue : 118, 122, 125
    Louis XVI (restaurant) :
    122
    Louvre : 28
    Madeleine (place de la) :
    118, 122, 126
    Malesherbes (boulevard) :
    19, 126
    Meurice (hotel) : 75
    Monceau (road) : 70
    Montmorency
    (Boulevard) : 71
    Pépinière (road) : 124
    Prunier : 126
    Ritz (hotel) : 118, 122,
    124
    Royale (road) : 118, 122
    Saint-Augustin (square) :
    125
    Tour d'Argent : 75
    Weber : 118
Raspelière (la) : 75
Réveillon : 66, 83, 84
Rivebelle : 108

Almond cake : 181
Apple tart : 178
Apricot tartlets : 177
Baked eggs : 139
Baked York ham : 159
Béarnaise sauce : 158
Beef braised in wine : 162
Boeuf Stroganoff : 160
Bouillabaisse : 145
Brill braised in cider : 144
Brill with white sauce : 150
Cabbage soup with dried bacon : 136
Calves' kidneys cooked in Cognac : 160
Carp in beer : 150
Carp with tomato : 149
Casserole of beef : 156
Casserole of veal : 162

Cheese soufflé : 140
Chestnut pudding : 185
Chocolate creams : 185
Chocolate soufflés : 180
Christmas pudding : 175
Coffee bavarois : 174
Currant cake : 182
Egg, tomato, anchovy and tuna salad : 140
Fish soup (see *Bouillabaisse*)
French bean salad : 137
Fricassee of chicken in Madeira and truffle sauce : 170
Fried gudgeon: 148
Grey mullet with cucumber : 154
Grilled crawfish in white sauce : 146
Grilled red mullet : 144

Grilled turbot with hollandaise sauce : 151
Hollandaise sauce : 151
Japanese salad : 138
Jellied beef : 158
Jugged hare : 164
Leg of lamb with béarnaise sauce : 156
Lobster American style : 148
Meat and vegetable broth : 163
Miniature brioches : 181
Miniature madeleines : 182
Muffins : 174
Mushroom, asparagus and chive omelette : 137
Partridges with champagne : 170

Peach compote : 172
Pineapple and truffle salad : 174
Poached bass : 154
Potato salad : 136
Rabbit with bacon : 166
Rice pudding with fruit : 180
Sauce gribiche : 158
Sauteed chicken : 167
Scrambled eggs with bacon : 135
Skate in black butter : 146
Sole in sea-food sauce : 142
Sponge cake : 178
Strawberry mousse : 172
Trout with almonds : 143
Vol-au-vents : 134
Wild duck with cranberries : 166

"Who cannot recall, as I can, the reading they did in the holidays, which one would conceal successively in all those hours of the day peaceful and inviolable enough to be able to afford it refuge. In the mornings, after returning from the park, when everyone had gone out for a walk, I would slip into the dining-room, where no one would be coming until the still distant hour for lunch except for the old, relatively silent Félicie."

QUOTATIONS

The excerpts from the works of Marcel Proust are drawn from the following editions:

Jean Santeuil, translated by Gerard Hopkins, Weidenfeld and Nicholson, London, 1955.

Against Sainte-Beuve, translated by John Sturrock, Penguin 1988.

Remembrance of Things Past, translated by K. Scott Moncrieff and Terence Kilmartin, Chatto and Windus 1981. Page references in this book refer to the Penguin 1989 edition.

The excerpts from *Monsieur Proust* by Céleste Albaret are taken from the Collins and Harvill 1976 edition, translated by Barbara Bray.

Francillon, A Drama in Three Acts, A. Dumas fils, Bean, Webley & Co. London, 1887.

FURTHER READING

Arlyck, Élisabeth Cardonne "Pièce montée et sorbets : Flaubert et Proust", *French Forum*, January 1978.

Brillat Savarin, Anthelme *Physiologie du Goût*, Flammarion, 1982.

Borrel, Anne "Les Cuisines de la Création", *Bulletin Marcel Proust 39*, Société des Amis de Marcel Proust et des Amis de Combray, 1989.

Borrel Anne, "Céleste and the Genius", *The UAB Marcel Proust Symposium*, edited by William C. Carter, Summa Publications, Birmingham, Alabama, 1989.

Courtine, Robert J. et Jean Desmur *Anthologie de la littérature gastronomique*, Les Écrivains à table, Trévise, 1970.

Da Costa, F. "La Cuisine et la table dans l'œuvre de Marcel Proust", *Bulletin de la Société des Amis de Marcel Proust et des Amis de Combray*, n° 26, 1976.

Deleuze, Gilles *Proust et les signes*, PUF, 1976.

De Man, *Allegories of reading. Figural lanugage in Rousseau, Nietzche, Rilke and Proust*, New Haven and London, Yale University Press, 1979.

Doubrovsky, Serge *La Place de La Madeleine*, Écriture et fantasme chez Proust, Mercure de France, 1974.

Escoffier, Auguste *Souvenirs inédits*, Flammarion, 1985.

Gilroy, James P. "Food, Cooking and Eating in Proust's *À la recherche du temps perdu*", *Twentieth Century Literature : A Scholarly and Critical Journal*, 33 (1), Spring 1987.

Girard, René *La Violence et le sacré*, Grasset 1972.

Gold, Arthur et Robert Fizdale "At the table-Taking Care of M. Proust", *House & Garden*, May 1983.

Gourdeau Wilson, Gabrielle "L'Immangeable repas proustien", *Bulletin de la Société des Amis de Marcel Proust et des Amis de Combray* n° 37, 1987.

Guillemard, Colette *La Fourchette et la plume*, 150 recettes de cuisine inspirées des œuvres d'écrivains célèbres, Carrère, 1988.

Haroche, Michel *Marcel Proust, Bulletin de la Société des Amis de Marcel Proust et des Amis de Combray*, n° 37, 1987.

King, Shirley *Dining with Marcel Proust*, A Practical Guide to French cuisine of the Belle Époque, Foreword by James Beard, Thames & Hudson, 1979.

Milly, Jean "L'Arrière-cuisine de Françoise" dans *Proust dans le texte et l'avant-texte*, Flammarion, 1985.

Monselet, Charles *La Cuisinière poétique*, Le Promeneur, 1988.

Montesquiou, Robert de *Prières de Tous*, Huit Dizains d'un Chapelet rythmiques, Dessins de Mme Madeleine Lemaire, Paris, "Maison du Livre", 1902.

Moulin, Léo *Les Liturgies de la table*, Albin Michel, 1988.

Pampille, *Les Bons plats de France*, Arthème Fayard.

Richard, Jean-Pierre "Proust et l'objet alimentaire", *Littérature* 6, 1972.

Richard, Jean-Pierre *Proust et le monde sensible*, Seuil, 1974.

Rivers, J.-E. *Proust & the Art of Love*, Columbia University Press, New York, 1980.

Robertson, Jane "The Relationship between the Hero and Françoise in *À la recherche du temps perdu*", *French Studies*, 25, 1971.

Sonnenfeld, Albert "Érotique Madeleine", *Kentucky Romance Quarterly*, 1969.

Urbain-Dubois, *La Cuisine d'aujourd'hui*, Flammarion, 1890.

Yoxall, H. W. "Wine and Food in Proust – A gastronomic review of *Remembrance of Things Past*", 1 – *Wine and food*, n° 119, Autumn 1963; 2 – *Wine and Food*, n° 120, Winter 1963.

TEXT

P. 10 : Against Sainte-Beuve p. 3 – **p. 11** : Time Regained p. 931 – **p. 15** : Jean Santeuil p. 97; Swann's Way pp. 50, 51, 41 – **p. 16** Swann's Way pp. 48, 50, 51 – **p. 18** : Swann's Way pp. 53, 54 – **p. 21** : Cities of the Plain pp. 968 Swann's Way p. 19 Jean Santeuil pp. 141, 90, 91 – **pp. 22–23** : Jean Santeuil p. 113, 197 Swann's Way p. 21, Jean Santeuil p. 132, Swann's Way p. 131, 77 Jean Santeuil p. 141 – **p. 28** : Swann's Way pp. 76, 77, 131 – **p. 30** : Swann's Way p. 132, 63, 86, 135 – **p. 33** : Jean Santeuil pp. 96, 97, 101, Swann's Way p. 119 – **p. 36** Swann's Way pp. 32, 36 – **p. 44** : Within a Budding Grove p. 638, Swann's Way pp. 215, 216, Within a Budding Grove p. 567, 591 – **p. 45** : Within a Budding Grove pp. 589, 619 – **p. 47** : Within a Budding Grove pp. 543, 545, 546 – **p. 50** : Swann's Way pp. 240, 241, 242, 243, 245, 246 – **p. 52** : Swann's Way p. 82 Within a Budding Grove pp. 579, 566, 567 – **p. 58** : Jean Santeuil pp. 451, 452, 471 The Guermantes Way p. 75 – **p. 59** : The Guermantes Way pp. 75, 78, 411 – **p. 60–61** : The Guermantes Way p. 97 – **p. 62** : The Guermantes Way pp. 97, 98 – **p. 66** : Swann's Way p. 206 – **p. 68** : Swann's Way pp. 280, 278 – **p. 69** : Swann's Way p. 277 – **p. 70** : Swann's Way pp. 278, 279 – **p. 71** : Swann's Way p. 226 Time Regained pp. 730, 731, 732 – **p. 75** : Time Regained p. 732 Cities of the Plain pp. 929, 930, 931, 962, 971 – **p. 76** : Cities of the Plain p. 971, 968 – **p. 83–84** : Jean Santeuil pp. 243, 244, 415, 417, 418 – **pp. 84–85** : Swann's Way p. 199 – **p. 85** : The Guermantes Way pp. 10, 11 – **p. 86** : The Guermantes Way p. 213 – **p. 90** : The Guermantes Way pp. 213, 214 – **pp. 90–92** : The Guermantes Way p. 532 – **p. 92** The Guermantes Way pp. 519, 520, 521, 522, 523, 524, 536 – **p. 94** : The Guermantes Way pp. 504, 505, 506 – **p. 100** : Within a Budding Grove pp. 711, 712, 713, 714, 715, 725, 726 – **p. 101** : Within a Budding Grove p. 727 – **p. 101–102** Within a Budding Grove p. 724, 725 – **p. 102** : Within a Budding Grove pp. 746, 747 – **p. 106** : Within a Budding Grove p. 929 – **pp. 106–107** : Within a Budding Grove p. 757 – **pp. 107–108** : Within a Budding Grove pp. 750, 751 – **pp. 108–109** : Within a Budding Grove p. 867 – **p. 109** : The Guermantes Way pp. 117, 118 – **p. 111** : Within a Budding Grove pp. 867, 868 – **p. 112** : Within a Budding Grove pp. 868, 869, 934, 935, 845, 846, 931, 932, 958, 965 – **p. 122** : The Guermantes Way p. 21 Céleste Albaret, Monsieur Proust p. 72 – **p. 124** : Céleste Albaret, Monsieur Proust pp. 72, 73 – **p. 126** : Céleste Albaret, Monsieur Proust p. 73, 78, 79 Cities of the Plain pp. 875, 876 Time Regained p. 924 – **p. 125** Céleste Albaret, Monsieur Proust p. 73 – **p. 126** : Céleste Albaret, Monsieur Proust p. 74 Time Regained p. 1091 Within a Budding Grove p. 480, 481 – **p. 128** : Within a Budding Grove p. 480, 522, 523 – **p. 129** : Time Regained p. 1095 – **p. 134** : The Guermantes Way p. 506 – **p. 136** : Jean Santeuil p. 418 Time Regained p. 731 – **p. 137** : Swann's Way p. 119 The Captive p. 124 – **p. 138** : Swann's Way p. 279 – **p. 139** : Jean Santeuil p. 90, 91 – **p. 140** : Within a Budding Grove pp. 727, 522 – **p. 142** : Swann's Way p. 279 – **p. 144** : Swann's Way p. 76 The Fugitive p. 646 – **p. 145** : Cities of the Plain p. 929 – **p. 146** : Against Sainte-Beuve; Chardin and Rembrandt p. 125 Cities of the Plain p. 931 – **p. 148** : Within a Budding Grove p. 579 Jean Santeuil p. 90 – **p. 149** : Jean Santeuil p. 122 – **p. 150** : Time Retained p. 731 – **p. 154** : Within a Budding Grove p. 861 The Guermantes Way p. 118 – **p. 156** : Swann's Way p. 11 The Guermantes Way p. 611 – **p. 158** : Swann's Way pp. 19, 21 Within a Budding Grove p. 480 – **p. 159** : Within a Budding Grove p. 480 – **p. 160** : The Captive p. 134 Within a Budding Grove p. 494 – **p. 162** : Within a Budding Grove p. 494 Swann's Way p. 119 – **p. 163** : Céleste Albaret, Monsieur Proust p. 73 – **p. 164** : Jean Santeuil p. 143 – **p. 166** : Within a Budding Grove pp. 521, 522, 832 – **p. 170** : The Guermantes Way p. 523 – **p. 172** : Cities of the Plain p. 971 – **p. 174** : Within a Budding Grove p. 495 Swann's Way p. 268 Within a Budding Grove p. 650 – **p. 175** : Within a Budding Grove p. 567 – **p. 177** : Within a Budding Grove p. 965 – **p. 178** : Against Sainte-Beuve p. 204 – **p. 180** : Within a Budding Grove p. 868 Swann's Way p. 79 – **p. 181** Swann's Way pp. 76, 77 – **p. 182** : Within a Budding Grove p. 546 Swann's Way p. 50 – **p. 185** : Swann's Way p. 77 Within a Budding Grove p. 502

CAPTIONS

P. 17 : Swann's Way p. 56 – **p. 19** : Swann's Way p. 70 – **p. 20** : Swann's Way pp. 56, 55 – **p. 23** : Jean Santeuil p. 110 – **p. 28** : Jean Santeuil p. 90 – **p. 32** : Swann's Way p. 131 – **p. 37** : Swann's Way p. 58, 77 – **p. 38** : Jean Santeuil p. 96, 97 Swann's Way p. 76 Jean Santeuil 197 – **p. 43** : Within a Budding Grove p. 637 Swann's Way p. 273 – **p. 47** : Swann's Way p. 243 Within a Budding Grove p. 546 – **p. 51** : Within a Budding Grove p. 546 – **p. 52** : Within a Budding Grove p. 545 – **p. 55** : Jean Santeuil p. 472 – **p. 60** : The Guermantes Way pp. 78, 97 – **p. 63** : Against Sainte-Beuve p. 124 – **p. 66** : Time Regained p. 730 – **p. 70** : The Captive p. 199 – **p. 74** : Jean Santeuil p. 270 – **p. 76** : Jean Santeuil p. 283 Swann's Way p. 337 – **p. 81** : Jean Santeuil p. 243 – **p. 84** : Jean Santeuil p. 178 – **p. 86** : Jean Santeuil p. 247 Time Regained p. 905 – **p. 90** : Jean Santeuil p. 244 – **p. 95** : Jean Santeuil p. 243 – **p. 99** : Within a Budding Grove p. 732, 777 – **p. 101** : Cities of the Plain p. 801 – **p. 103** : Time Regained p. 908 Against Sainte-Beuve p. 124 – **p. 107** : Within a Budding Grove p. 894 – **p. 108** : Jean Santeuil p. 154 – **p. 111** : Cities of the Plain p. 1002 Within a Budding Grove 760 – **p. 112** : Jean Santeuil pp. 149, 154 – **p. 117** : Jean Santeuil p. 474 – **p. 118** : Jean Santeuil p. 91 – **p. 122** : Within a Budding Grove p. 494 – **p. 126** : Within a Budding Grove p. 502 – **p. 135** : Jean Santeuil p. 243 – **p. 139** : Against Sainte-Beuve p. 124 – **p. 141** : Swann's Way p. 131 – **p. 147** : Cities of the Plain p. 931 – **p. 151** : Within a Budding Grove p. 965 – **p. 165** : Against Sainte-Beuve; Chardin and Rembrandt p. 124 – **p. 176** : Jean Santeuil p. 149 – **p. 178** : Jean Santeuil p. 153 – Jean Santeuil p. 149 – **p. 183** : Swann's Way p. 242 – **p. 189** : Against Sainte-Beuve p. 195–6.

ACKNOWLEDGEMENTS

We would not have been able to take the photographs in this book without the help of a large number of people.

I would like to express my sincere gratitude to all who have offered their friendship, advice and enthusiasm, willingly entrusting me with precious artefacts so that I could create the desired settings and moods: Daphné de Saint Sauveur, Alexandra de Caraman-Chimay, Jean-Louis de Maigret, Marc de Ferrière, curator of the Musée Christofle, Jacques Bontillot, curator of the Musée de Montereau, Jean de Rohan Chabot, Olivier Gaube de Gers, Madame Arnaud, M., Mme and Mlle Bouniol de Gineste, M. and Mme de La Conte, Anne Gayet, Annick Clavier, Armand Ventilo, Au Bon Usage, Au Passé Retrouvé, Au Puceron Chineur, Aux Fils du Temps, Beauté Divine, Bleu Passé, boutiques Descamps, Cassegrain, Christian Benais, Christian Dior, Claudine Peltot, Constance Maupin, Cristal d'Arques, cristallerie de Baccarat, cristallerie de St-Louis, Dîners en Ville, Eric Dubois/Art Domestique ancien, faïencerie de Gien, Fanette, Fauchon, Foncegrive, galerie Didier Ludot, galerie Dominique Paramythiotis, galerie G. Bernard, galerie Loft, Josy Broutin, Argenterie des Francs-Bourgeois, Boutique Georges Pesle, Boutique Magnolia, la Châtelaine, la Galerie Pittoresque au Louvre des Antiquaires, la Maison Opéra, la Tuile à Loup, la Vaisselle, le Cochelin au Louvre des Antiquaires, les Bijoux du Louvre des Antiquaires, Les Deux Orphelines, les etablissements Morand, les tissus Lelièvre, Liliane François, Madame est servie, Marie-José Bauemer, Madeleine Gely, Muriel Grateau, orfévrerie Christofle and the Musée Christofle, orfévrerie Odiot, orfévrerie Puiforcat, Point à la ligne, porcelaine Bernardaud, porcelaine Haviland & Parlon, porcelaine Raynaud, Primrose Bordier for le Jacquard français, Siècle, Un Jardin en plus, Une Maison à Paris.

My special thanks to:
Pierre Ermé, chief confectioner at Fauchon's who, with great enthusiasm and flair, created the superb cakes and pastries;
Marianne Robic and Monsieur François, for their magnificent floral compositions;
Hubert Avilès and the kitchen staff at the Pullman Grand Hotel, Cabourg, who prepared the dishes for the "At the Seaside" chapter;
Jean-Jacques Aubert and Anne-Françoise Pelissier, who have assisted me throughout and whose generosity, energy and efficiency have been quite outstanding.

Editions du Chêne would like to thank the staff of the Laboratoire Nouveau Gorne for their friendly cooperation in developing the films.

PHOTOGRAPHIC CREDITS

Bridgeman Giraudon: p. 19
Caisse Nationale des Monuments Historiques et des Sites:
pp. 45, 81 (top), 83, 129
Bernard Fiévet: p. 15
Giraudon: pp. 32, 99 (top; ADAGP)
Hachette: pp. 45 (bottom), 65 (top), 94, 101, 125
René Jacques: p. 109
Lauros-Giraudon: p. 85; ADAGP
Louis Monier: p. 133
Musée Marcel Proust: pp. 16, 18, 31, 47, 117 (top)
Musées Royaux des Beaux-Arts de Belgique: p. 43 (top)
Réunion des Musées Nationaux: pp. 63, 103, 139, 161
Roger-Viollet: pp. 55, 59, 70
Scala: p. 60
Studio Lourmel: p. 165
Wallraf-Richartz Museum, Cologne: p. 171

Printed in Italy by G. Canale & C. S.p.A. - Borgaro T.se - Torino